SO LONGS MY SOUL

HEART-CRY FOR INTIMACY WITH GOD

As the deer pants for the water brooks, so pants my soul for You, O God. My soul thirsts for God, for the living God. *Psalm 42:1, 2*

As pants the hart for cooling streams, When heated in the chase;
So longs my soul, O God, for Thee, And thy refreshing grace.

- Nahum Tate, 1652-1715
- Nicholas Brady, 1659-1726

So Longs My Soul

Heart-cry for Intimacy with God

Rod Taylor

So Longs My Soul by Rod Taylor
Copyright ©2020 by Rod Taylor
All Rights Reserved.
ISBN: 978-1-59755-608-8
Published by: ADVANTAGE BOOKS™ Longwood, Florida, USA

All Scripture quotations, unless otherwise noted, taken from the New King James Version® (NKJV®) Copyright ©1979, 1980, 1982 by Thomas Nelson, Inc. Used by permission. All rights reserved.

Scripture quotations marked AV taken from The Holy Bible, Authorized King James Version.

Scripture quotations marked NIV taken from the Holy Bible, New International Version® NIV®. Copyright ©1973, 1978, 1984, 2011 by Biblica, Inc©. Used by permission of Biblica, Inc©. All rights reserved worldwide.

Scripture quotations marked NLT taken from the *Holy Bible*, New Living Translation, copyright ©1996, 2004, 2007 by Tyndale House Foundation. Used by permission Tyndale House Publishers, Inc., Carol Stream, IL 60188. All rights reserved.

Scripture quotations marked CEV taken from the Contemporary English Version, copyright ©1995, American Bible Society. Used by permission. All rights reserved.

Scripture quotations marked The Message taken from THE MESSAGE. Copyright© 1993, 1994, 1995, 1996, 2000, 2001, 2002. Used by permission of NavPress Publishing group.

Scripture quotations marked TPT taken from The Passion Translation. Copyright© 2017, 2018 by BroadStreet Publishing Group, LLC. Used by permission. All rights reserved. The Passion Translation.com

Scripture quotations marked PHILLIPS, taken from The New Testament in Modern English by J.B. Phillips ©1960, 1972 J.B. Phillips. Administered by The Archbishops' Council of the Church of England. Used by permission.

Library of Congress Catalog Number: 2020919115

First Printing: November 2020
20 21 22 23 24 25   10 9 8 7 6 5 4 3 2 1
Printed in the United States of America

I dedicate this book to my heavenly Father, who has drawn me to the embrace of his breathtaking, boundless love. He has called me to an amazing adventure of his will and a life-fulfilling, divine romance with Christ.

I dedicate this book to my beautiful, remarkable wife who has traveled with me on this incredible journey, the one who sent my heart racing the first time I saw her and still sends my heart racing after all of these years. Thank you, Marlene. This book would not have been possible without you in my life. This book is ours together.

I dedicate this book to all of the godly men and women whose passionate love for Jesus has set my heart ablaze with a consuming desire to know Christ intimately and to love him supremely.

I write this book to my children and grandchildren. I love you, dearly. My desire and prayer are that you will always walk in the abundant life in Christ, always joy in the astonishing, endless adventure of doing God's will, and always rest in his amazing love.

I write this book to all those who passionately long to know Christ more intimately, who desire to plunge more deeply into his fathomless love, who pant for God as the deer pants for the water brooks.

So Longs My Soul

Contents

Introduction

There is a genuine and growing thirst in our world for God himself. Even among God's people, there is a holy discontent. People are not satisfied with being religious or with the acceptance of doctrine alone. People desire an intimate relationship with the living, personal God.

The greatest privilege we could ever have is knowing and loving God. The deepest joy we could ever possess is experiencing his matchless, measureless love now and for eternity. The most sublime wonder we could ever know is the inexpressible wonder of intimate fellowship with God. Each of us can step into the reality of knowing God in a profound, personal relationship. Surely our hearts must respond in worship and complete consecration to such an amazing God who gives such a call and offers such a privilege.

God calls us to himself and the abundant life for which he created us. If we respond to God with open hearts, overwhelming hunger for his presence, and honesty concerning our spiritual need, we can experience all that God offers. When we approach God with childlike awe about who he is and genuine expectation that he will fulfill his promises for us, he will not disappoint us. God will give us overflowing life that will pour through us to this love-starved, life-seeking, wounded world.

God promises that if we seek him, we shall surely find him, when we seek him with all our hearts (Jer. 29:13). If we continue to seek him, we will continue to discover him in ever-increasing fullness. God assures us that if we love him with a passionate, life-surrendering love that propels us into trusting obedience, he will manifest himself to us as he makes his home with us (John 14:21, 23). What more significant promise could we ever receive? What more life-changing experience could we have than to know God intimately and participate in his eternal purposes? This greatest blessing is possible only because of God's amazing grace and Christ's triumphant work on the cross.

I present these reflections on knowing and loving God as an offering to my heavenly Father. I offer these words to those who desire to plunge ever deeper into the fathomless love of God and those who long to experience the extraordinary adventure of God's divine will. I write to those who thirst and pant for God as the deer pants for flowing streams and invite you on this journey with me. Let's find and live that which alone will fully satisfy the longing of our hearts.

I realize that extraordinary men and women of God with far deeper insights and experiences of God have written many profound and excellent books. However, if you read each chapter of this book as if I were writing to you, we could have a conversation together about our desire to know personally this astonishing God who calls us to himself.

People who read these words may come from different ecclesiastical backgrounds. I have not written to support one doctrinal position over another. Through the centuries, Bible-believing men and women of various theological persuasions have had the same passionate desire to know God intimately, experience his incomparable love personally, and then express this love to the world. Our hunger for God and the fulfillment we find in his presence, love, and will are at the heart of biblical truth. I encourage you to read with a sincere and childlike desire to explore the wonder of knowing God and walking in his amazing love.

Will you pray as you read, as I have prayed as I have written, that these reflections on knowing and loving God will open our lives in a more significant way to the limitless, unfailing, fiery love of God? May our hearts be set ablaze with a growing passion for knowing and loving God as never before! We are called to an abundant life which glorifies our worthy Savior and Lord. This life can be ours.

"Heavenly Father, take these words I have written. Anoint them. Envelop them in your divine presence. Fill these written words with your Holy Spirit of love and power. Use them to stir seeking, thirsting hearts to pursue their longing for you. Use these words, Lord, to encourage souls that long and pant for you as the deer pants for streams of water. May we, who thirst, experience you in ever-increasing fullness! Take us, Lord, deeper into your loving heart, in Christ's name."

Chapter 1

I Want to Know Christ in Intimate Communion

A few years ago, someone paid thousands of dollars for the kidney stone of a movie and television celebrity. The things people value can be shallow, shameful, or even silly.

Prowlers once broke into a large department store. They didn't steal anything. What they did was to switch the price tags all around. (This was before stores marked items with computer codes for scanning.) They tagged expensive items with much lower costs and inexpensive articles with exorbitant prices. Can you imagine the confusion in the morning before people discovered the price changes? Some people got real bargains while others got soundly swindled.

What is crazier, more serious, is that people can have their values and priorities in this life all mixed up. Many miss the joy, adventure, and fulfillment of life because they don't know what is truly valuable. It's like someone got into the world, into our lives, and switched all the price tags. Everything is confused. People don't know what ultimately matters in this world.

The Apostle Paul knew what was of real value, and he knew what he wanted. While Paul was in prison, perhaps not knowing whether he would face martyrdom, he wrote a letter to the church at Philippi. Paul desired to send a vital message to a church that he dearly loved, especially if these were his last words written to them. *"For I want you to understand what really matters"* (Phil. 1:10 NLT), he told them. Paul wanted the church to know what was of real value, and so he wrote: *"But what things were gain to me, these have I counted loss for Christ. Yet indeed I also count all things loss for the excellence of the knowledge of Christ Jesus my Lord, for whom I have suffered the loss of all things, and count them as rubbish, that I may gain Christ."* (Phil. 3:7-8). *"But Christ has shown me that what I once thought was valuable is worthless. Nothing is as wonderful as knowing Christ Jesus my Lord."* (Phil. 3:8 CEV). *"I want to know Christ"* (Phil. 3:10 NIV).

The truth in these passages of God's Word is so profound that we could never get to the end of all the meaning that it holds. If we consider just the statement of Paul, "I want to know Christ," we find a pathway to the heart of God and the center of true Christianity. Paul considered everything else "loss," "garbage," "rubbish," "dung," "that I may know him." "I want to know Christ!" was Paul's longing and heart-cry.

Here was a man, Paul, a Pharisee of Pharisees. Concerning the righteousness which is in the law, he was blameless (Phil. 3:6). He had been a leader in religion, but now he still says, "I want to know Christ."

We can attend church. We can have a head knowledge of God's Word. We can go through the motions in word and ritual. We can play religion and never come to an intimate relationship with Jesus Christ. We can be religious and never really know Christ or know him to the level that Jesus paid such a price that we might experience. Shallow or self-centered religion can harden us to the real walk with God to which he calls us.

Even after Paul's remarkable conversion to true faith in Christ, he continued longing for a more intimate relationship with him. Paul had accomplished many good things for Christ. He had established churches, completed daring exploits, and God had saved and healed many under his ministry. Yet Paul was not impressed with himself. His longing was still, "I want to know Christ."

When persecuted, beaten with whips and rods, stoned, and shipwrecked, Paul did not resent it. He did not give up. He still declared his heart aspiration to be: "I want to know Christ."

Now, Paul writes these words while he is in prison. He was not a young man anymore. He could have just been satisfied with his past accomplishments and coasted home. But he still proclaims as his greatest desire, "I want to know Christ." Paul knew what was of paramount value.

When we look at the word used by Paul regarding "knowing" Christ, we find special meaning from the original language that reveals something of the depth of Paul's passion and longing. *"To know Christ,"* as Paul desires and declares, is to know Christ personally, to know the Lord Jesus by experience through intimate companionship and communion with him. This knowing is not just knowing about someone. This relationship is not casual knowing. Paul is saying, "I want to know Christ in intimate, personal experience." Paul does not want just to know about Christ—not even only as Savior in the forgiveness of sin. He wants to know Christ in the deepest kind of spiritual relationship. Paul longs to love Christ passionately and be embraced by the immeasurable, transforming love of God.

There is a place where knowing God is so real, his love and presence are so profoundly and overwhelmingly experienced, that it is beyond language to express. His presence can be like a fire within us that seems it would melt our hearts as wax in the flames of his love. The awareness of God's presence may be realized as the Word of God becoming supernaturally alive within us, or a great peace of spirit, which is God's peace, or a glorious unspeakable, supernatural joy. God's presence can be perceived as a breathtaking love that overwhelms us, transforms us, and woos us to an even deeper immersion into his fathomless love. God may manifest himself to us as a great desire for holiness—a heart of resolve for doing his will—a strength or courage beyond our own—a rise of great, God-born faith and expectancy—a definite sense of his guidance—a recognition of the truths of God and his ways being the ultimate answer to life's questions and being worthy of full allegiance—a rapturous revelation of who God is in His holiness, majesty, and all the glory of his perfections—a heartfelt, intense longing for those without Christ to know his saving grace or for Christians and the church to live in the fullness of God's purpose and power, or a sublime and indescribable but undeniably real, spiritual perception that God is present with us and within us.

The wondrous manifestations of God's presence to the awareness of his children are as limitless and varied as the manifold dimensions of his character and as real and deep as the need and longing of every human heart. In this holy place of communion with God, we come to know his heart. And though not continually experienced in such glory, our deep relationship with God can be sustained and nurtured by faith and obedience to his Word and the Holy Spirit.

The conscious awareness of God's presence is more than just our sensual perception of the natural world, or our natural emotions, or our mental constructs based on logical presuppositions. This conscious awareness of God can, and often does, manifest itself as divine love. Our conscious awareness of God and his love originates in our spirits, where God meets with us. God's love abiding within us can be recognized and understood as God's presence at work. As we are broken in our dependence upon ourselves, God's presence and love are released outward through us to this love-starved world.

In our seeking to love God supremely, we should recognize that any experience of God or revelation of God that does not align with God's Word is a false experience and no true knowing of God. We are not to seek for "experiences." Seeking spiritual experiences can lead to deceit and darkness by the enemy. We are to pursue God himself, in Christ, because we know that our heart's longing can only be satisfied in Christ alone. Only by Christ, and from the place of his presence, can we live in a way that pleases and glorifies him.

In this intimate relationship with life itself, his grace and the glory of his presence change us into his likeness (2 Cor. 3:18). God's presence transforms our hearts into a tabernacle of his habitation and changes our lives into the beautiful expression of who he meant us to be. Then, God sends us into the world with the good news of the abundant life in Christ.

Prayer is such a precious, beautiful, and longed-for act of worship for those who love God and long to know him more deeply. Prayer is an especially significant and sacred place of our intimate meeting with God. Here love meets Love, and here we are transformed into the unique and beautiful persons that Christ created us to be. Here we are called to participate in his eternal purposes through intercessory prayer. Such fiery, Holy-Spirit-enabled communion opens heaven upon us and releases divine light and love to us and through us to this needy world. The place of prayer is especially precious and longed for by God himself, who desires to share himself with us in the wonder-filled fellowship of his Holy love.

The knowing of God in such holy communion is more than a feeling, more than fleshly emotions. This relationship is about the impact of the very Spirit of God upon our spirits. God, who once dwelt in radiant glory in the holy of holies in the tabernacle, now chooses to dwell within us with the same glorious presence. This divine romance is about our hearts' fixed attention to devote ourselves to God and his revealed Word.

Our knowing of God is not a mystical experience empty of the truth revealed in God's Word. This intimate relationship with God is about the truths concerning God—who he is and what he has done for us—being made real and life-transforming by the Holy Spirit's presence. God's Holy Spirit does not annihilate or absorb our spirits. God's presence enhances our unique personalities, so we become beautiful, creative, fulfilled people.

On the last and great day of the Feast of Tabernacles, the priests carried pitchers of water to the Temple. This act was a ritual celebration of the water that miraculously and abundantly burst forth from the rock in the desert to satisfy the children of Israel's thirst. Just as the priests were passing him in this celebration, Jesus stood and cried with a loud voice, *"... If anyone thirsts, let him come to Me and drink. He who believes in Me, as the Scripture has said, out of his heart (innermost being) will flow rivers of living water. But this He spoke concerning the Spirit"* (John 7:37-39). Such is the marvel and mystery of God making himself known to us! Oh, the awesome wonder, the inexpressible privilege of fellowship with God! We can have this astonishing relationship with God as we open our hearts to him because he opened his heart to us. We give ourselves entirely to him because he gave himself utterly to us.

This knowing of God is an inner revelation and communion with God, the Creator himself. God's Holy Spirit within us makes us closer to him than a relationship with any other person. This relationship with God is an abiding in Christ that stirs, converts, and reorders our lives in a real way that becomes a beautiful and powerful demonstration to the world of the transforming love and grace of God. It is Christ in us, and we in Christ in a sublime bond of love. Our relationship with God is truly and literally and gloriously God's Spirit in our spirits, bringing us to the fullness of our calling and our faith, all for the glory of his name.

At the place of knowing God intimately, his presence and love overtake us and overwhelm us. We long to pour out our lives as an offering. We come to a place in our relationship with God where nothing else matters, yet where, because of this new-perspective relationship, everything else and everyone else now matter in an entirely new and more significant way. Our longing to know Christ can be so great that it surpasses every other longing and focuses, shapes, and energizes everything we do. God is life and fire within us. God melts, molds, guides, transforms, enables, empowers, and overwhelms us with his love.

This relationship is not with an impersonal force. We commune with the person of Christ himself who is with us and within us by the Holy Spirit. Here our lives are lived out from fellowship with God, lived out from the place of his presence every day in every circumstance. God's truth and grace captivate us, and we are compelled by our experience of his love to share the good news of such abundant life with others.

This divine fellowship with God is not just for an elite group of super-spiritual people. God invites everyone to this intimate communion with him. Our life-fulfilling fellowship with our Creator is possible, not because of any ascetic techniques on our part, but because of Christ's gracious and mediating work. This personal relationship with God is at the heart of authentic, vital Christianity.

Jesus lived a life of unbroken fellowship with God the Father. By the grace and help of God, we can live such a life as well. We may not do it perfectly in this life—and we probably will not—but God meets us at the place of our authentic hunger and satisfies our longing. What could ever be a more wonder-filled privilege or ever be of higher value?

Knowing God in an intimate relationship is a place of true belonging, eternal significance, and incomparable hope. It is also a place where we profoundly bless God. This blessed life is what God won for us by his crucifixion, resurrection, ascension to the Father, and the sending of his Holy Spirit. God invites us to this knowledge of him, this loving relationship. Oh, what a glorious invitation! How can our hearts but cry, "I want to know Christ!"

Although we may not always have a conscious awareness of God's manifested presence, by faith, we believe the promise of God's real presence with us and within us. We can rest assured in God's pledge of intimate fellowship with us if we are truly hungry for God himself and longing to glorify his name. We can keep our hearts continually cleansed and clear with God through faith in Christ's atoning work on the cross. This intimate relationship is possible at any given moment for every man and woman through repentance and God's forgiving, life-giving grace.

The sad and tragic truth is that many Christians settle for less than God intends and desires for his children. We can be content with less than that for which Paul so ardently longed. The knowing of God in a profound, personal relationship is that for which he created us. We must not settle for less. Jesus paid a high price that we could have this fullest experience of life and joy with him. Christ gave his life in an atoning work on the cross so we would be forgiven and justified before God. God forgave and justified us so he could remove the barriers of sin that separated us from him. God removed those barriers so we could be united with him in an intimate communion of love forever. This glorious fellowship was God's desire and his grace-saturated plan all along.

We can now know by faith in God's promise, and by our experience, what is of real value. Now we can declare with Paul, "I want to know Christ," and find this fellowship with God to be ours and ours in ever-increasing fullness.

Chapter 2

I Want to Know Christ in Union with His Will

Paul's heart-cry was "to know Christ." "*I want to know Christ,*" he wrote to the Philippian church (Phil. 3:10 NIV). Paul wanted more than to know about Christ. He longed to know Christ intimately in real, personal experience. But by this declaration, Paul also meant something more. To know Christ means to know him concerning his will and purposes. Paul longed to be fully aware of and personally tuned to God's heart—to be in line with his aims in this world.

This understanding of the word "*know*" echoes the Old Testament use of the word as it refers to the acknowledgment of and obedience to God's revelation. To know Christ means to align ourselves with the desires of his heart. For Isaiah, Jeremiah, and others of the prophets, to know God was to be aware of his will and be willing to obey. Paul's union with Christ meant union with his will and purposes. If we want to know Christ as Paul longed to know him, as God calls us to know him, we will want to do his will.

We can miss God's call to us. We can want to know God's feel-good presence or desire to experience an easing of our guilty conscience and still live our self-willed lives. You and I can try to use God to fulfill our selfish ambitions or our power needs. We can seek his help in trouble, but not strive to know and do his will in our lives.

God can be an add-on to our lives—nothing more—like adding an extra room to our house where we can go when we need to be cheered up. We can want God like a rabbit's foot charm to bring us good luck, or like a hula girl on our car's dashboard. People tap the hula girl and make her dance when they want good luck. We can try to use Jesus and touch him, so he might dance for us and make everything happen according to our self-centered desires.

God must be more than this. He desires us to know him as the Lord of our lives. His heart and will for us are always for our eternal good and his eternal glory. To be aligned with God's will, to be in union with his purposes is more than just our acknowledgment of his forgiveness of our sins and then going our way, living our own lives as if God has no specific will for us to do or purpose for us to accomplish. Forgiveness of sins is just the beginning of a wonder-filled walk with God. This is a path of a personal relationship with our heavenly Father and a daily, vital, adventurous obedience to his ever-unfolding plans for our lives. God wants to lead us not only in the big decisions of our lives. God is interested in every detail of our lives. God desires to fill each day with the wonder of his presence and life-fulfilling participation in his divine purposes.

Each day God has a plan and an important assignment for us. In our Christian walk of love and obedience, our lives should be all about the present and the coming kingdom of God. We are to seek first God's kingdom, where his will is being done on earth as it is in heaven (Matt. 6:10). We find our most abundant blessings, our deepest meaning, and our greatest joy in this way of obedience to God's Word and his Spirit. God's Word reveals to us his heart, his will for our living, and his desire for us to share his life with the world. God wants to guide us by his holy and inspired Word and by the leading and checks of his Spirit every day. This way of obedience to God's guidance is how God chooses to accomplish his kingdom purposes in this world. This daily obedience is what makes our Christian life an exciting, ever-new adventure.

Our Christian walk is to be a daily, dynamic communion with God in which he speaks to us through his Word and the promptings of his Holy Spirit. The guidance of the Holy Spirit will always be in line with God's Word. This daily obedience to God is an essential and exciting part of the real adventure of true Christianity. We awaken in the morning to the thrill of what God might have for us in this new day, where he may take us as we trust and obey him in all circumstances of plans or providence. We begin the day with the expectant joy of fellowship with God and the genuine excitement of "What do you have for me to do today, heavenly Father? How can I please and glorify you? How can I share your love?" Our daily, moment by moment walk with God is a life of obedience to his grace-filled Word and his loving Spirit. This obedience fills our lives with the overflowing love of God that reveals him to those around us.

Our obedience to God will lead us to even more intimate communion with Christ as we follow in his steps. Jesus said, *"He who has My commandments and keeps them, it is he who loves Me. And he who loves Me will be loved by My Father, and I will love him and manifest Myself to him"* (John 14:21).

God may lead us in ways we don't foresee or understand, but it is always for our best and fulfills his gracious purposes. This life of coming after Jesus is the life of the greatest eternal blessing.

God is waiting with a holy, purpose-filled longing for those who will love him deeply. God is seeking those who will so dedicate themselves to him in utmost trust that they will listen for his guidance, do his will, and bring forth his present kingdom's purpose to bring life to this world.

God has a great blessing and an astounding adventure for us along this way of obedience to his will, but we must be God's without reservation. To fully come after Jesus means we must deny ourselves, deny our own will when contrary to God's will. God, who calls us to obedience, will be there with us by the Holy Spirit to enable us. Our call is to turn our hearts to him in sincere, prideless, and passionate aspiration to follow him. We acknowledge our weakness and place ourselves entirely in his hands. We trust in his promise to help us, and, by God's grace-given intervening power, choose to take ourselves off the throne of our hearts so that he might reign supreme in his rightful place. Along the way of obedience to a holy and loving God, we find our most complete freedom, our most fruitful fulfillment, and our most authentic selves because the will of God always brings us to his best.

God is looking for a person or group of people who will genuinely and joyfully love him, trust him, and obey him. He will come into their hearts with his overwhelming, overflowing presence. This group of people could fulfill, in power and fruitfulness, God's supreme mission and our great commission, to bring saving grace and abundant life to the world. This work of God would be a real, spiritual revival for a person or a group of people for God's glory. This wonder-filled experience of life is the aim of knowing God. To genuinely know God is to know him in union with his will.

When Paul declared, "I want to know Christ," he meant that he wanted to know Christ in intimate fellowship, and he desired to align his life with God's will and purposes. Paul's life demonstrated this longing. Our lives exhibit this hunger for God and his glory when our desire is truly to know Christ in union with his will.

Chapter 3

I Want to Know Christ in Ever-Increasing Fullness

Paul wrote a letter to the church at Philippi in which he declared, *"I want to know Christ"* (Phil. 3:10 NIV). By this, he meant that he wanted to know Christ in an intimate, personal relationship and that he wanted to know Christ in union with his will and purposes. However, the verb tense of the word *knowing* that Paul used reveals that this is a progressive knowing. Paul was saying I want to know Christ more and more in an ever-increasing fullness. Paul wrote that he had not yet apprehended it all, but that he was pressing on for this upward call of God in Christ Jesus (Phil. 3:13, 14).

This ever-increasing knowing of Christ is a part of the joy and exciting adventure of our walk with God. God desires to be continually disclosing more and more of himself and his plans to us. God's heart is ever unfolding to us as we unfold our hearts to him. There is no end to discovering the depth of his love and grace.

We taste God's goodness and love, the wonder and the glory of his very presence, and we are satisfied. Yet, the savor of him is so captivating and inexpressibly compelling that we desire to know him even more.

Paul was in prison. He was older now, but he still wanted to know God in even greater measure. "I press on," he said. "I reach with all that is within me for the upward call." Paul was not speaking about reaching for salvation as the new birth. Paul was already a Christian. He was writing about the knowing of God and his purposes. Paul writes, *"I press on, that I may lay hold of that for which Christ Jesus has also laid hold of me"* (Phil. 3:12). God lays hold of us so that we can lay hold of him in a real fellowship of love and divine purpose. This fellowship is not just some ecstatic, emotional experience that we seek, but God himself and the wonder and the glory of his presence.

Why should we hunger for more of God, to know him in a more significant way? Because God desires it. The omnipotent God who created all things out of nothing, who counts the number of the stars and calls them all by name (Ps. 147:4), loves us with measureless, unfailing, sacrificial love. Our heavenly Father desires to know us in ever-increasing fullness. What greater motivation would we need to hunger for more of him?

We should hunger to know God in an ever-expanding measure because our growth in him means a growing fulfillment of our lives. God wants this for us. God made us for himself and his purposes, and there is no true life apart from fellowship with God. God, himself, is our greatest joy and fulfillment. Would God create the universe for romance, prepare a bride for Christ, and not desire to know us in an intimate relationship? We hunger for more of God because he calls us to know him intimately. He stands at the door of our hearts and knocks that we might open the door and let him in for this holy fellowship of love. *"Behold, I stand at the door and knock. If anyone hears My voice and opens the door, I will come in to him and dine with him, and he with Me"* (Rev. 3:20). What a sacred feast of intimate love he offers to share with us! God could make us no higher offer. We could experience no greater joy or fulfillment.

We should seek to know Christ in an ever-deepening relationship for the sake of the world and the world's need. The world's greatest need, the world's only hope, is to live within God's loving purposes and find fulfillment in his loving embrace. We can only offer what we have. The world will see Jesus in us as we truly know him. Only by this can we show him to others in a way that opens hearts to his grace. To know Christ in this personal way is to experience the power of the resurrection (Phil. 3:10), and in the power of the resurrection, we can reveal him to others.

We should seek to know Christ because he is worthy to be pursued. No one or nothing else is so deserving of our devotion and the commitment of our lives. God is the one who gives value to all of creation. Apart from him, nothing has eternal significance, but in him and by him, all existence carries the meaning of his loving character and eternal plans. Only in knowing Christ, only from his presence and perspective, can we know all other things in their true meaning and value.

To seek to know God in ever-increasing fullness is for God's pleasure and glory. This truth is truly amazing! God desires to know each of us in this communion of love. We can say, "I want to know Christ", but God is saying, "I want to know *you*. I want to know you in an intimate relationship." How astounding, how almost incomprehensible is this that the almighty Creator ties his heart to our hearts? When we desire to know Christ, when we delight in his presence, this brings him pleasure and glorifies him. For us to want to respond to God's love and return his love, pleases him greatly.

I remember when I received a new and overwhelming revelation of my heavenly Father's love. I was holding our infant son, Timothy. He smiled back at me for the first time in recognition and delight. I remember the joy and pleasure I felt in his joy and pleasure in me. Suddenly, I had a revelation of how my heavenly Father feels about me and my response to him. My Father delights in me when I delight in him. When we are most delighted in God is when he is most glorified in us. Do we want to glorify God, then let's delight in him above all else. God says to us, "I want to know you."

We see this in the heart of God over and over in his Word. God finally and passionately proclaimed it at Calvary in his sacrificial display of love. God is still reaching for us today. He calls us each morning. He calls us throughout each day to surrender to his incomparable, immeasurable love. Our response to this reach of God determines everything. God created us to know him. Sin separated us from this embrace of God. Christ's atoning work on the cross made a way when it seemed there was no way. God removed the barriers. He spanned the gulf. Now we can know God in intimate fellowship. Now we can come home to the arms of God. This divine romance is the purpose of all creation.

How could one not be thrilled and overcome with inexpressible joy and thanksgiving at the discovery of such a God of boundless love! I was once an atheist, but God reached over my blindness and rebellion, and drew me to himself in love and called me to the fullness of life in him. How could I not be stirred to the depth of my soul to know Christ genuinely?

His possibilities in Christ stirred Paul. He was in prison, facing possible execution. Still, his joy was genuine, and his passion ablaze as he wrote to those at Philippi challenging them to know what is of preeminent value—knowing God and his will in ever-increasing fullness. He wrote I count all things as loss *"compared to the surpassing greatness of knowing Christ Jesus my Lord"* (Phil. 3:8 NIV).

Two ideas are key here: vision and passion. You see this in Paul's heartfelt statement. Paul had a view of what matters most. God may bless us with material things over which we are to be stewards, but Paul had a vision here for the eternal, spiritual kingdom of God, an aspiration for what is of supreme value. We also sense Paul's great passion: "I want to know Christ." This passion was the fiery and holy longing of his heart! We, too, can have this vision and this passion which lay hold of God.

How do we get to know God in this way? Jesus opened the door for us at Calvary and now gives us the invitation. The invitation is to accept our access into his presence because of Christ's atoning work on the cross. The call is to lose our lives for his sake that we might find our authentic lives in fullness in him (Matt. 16:25). We get to know him in ever-increasing fullness by responding when he calls; when he comes to our heart and invites us deeper into his love. *"When you said, 'Seek My Face,' My heart said to you, 'Your face, Lord, I will seek'"* (Ps. 27:8). When God comes and asks for our heart, our love, and our lives in fuller consecration, we say yes and surrender ourselves to him. This response of surrender is not just at our conversion experience, but every day of our lives after conversion.

Consider some of God's men and women recorded in God's Word: Abraham, Debra, Samuel, David, Elijah, Isaiah, Mary, the mother of Jesus, John the Baptist, Mary of Bethany, Peter, John, Paul. They were people just like you and me, but all of them were very different from one another. Peter's personality was not like John's. Elijah was not like Isaiah. Yet all knew God in intimate fellowship. What was the secret? Did they did have something in common? Although they were all different, they did have one thing in common. It was this: when they sensed God's approach and when they felt the call of God, they did something about it. That's the secret—simple but profound. When God drew near, when he reached for them, when he called for them to know him, they responded. They said yes to his invitation to intimacy. Then they nurtured this relationship until it became the most significant thing in their lives. You and I can respond to this call of God.

At conversion, God calls each of us to respond to him. After conversion, God continually gives us the invitation to know him in a more in-depth and vibrant fellowship and follow him in daily obedience. We can choose to say yes to this incomparable call continually, or we can refuse his invitation. We are often not sensitive or responsive to his call because we have given our affections first to other things. However, if we would surrender our lives to love God first, above all other things, and lose our lives to follow him in all his ways, we would find our lives enriched with eternal meaning. We would have blessings far greater than the temporary treasures of this world. We can experience this ever-deepening, ever-expanding relationship with our God. We can grow in our relationship with God as the Apostle Peter challenges us to "*grow in the grace and knowledge of our Lord and Savior Jesus Christ*" (2 Pet. 3:18).

This increasingly intimate walk with God is the most exciting, most fulfilling adventure to which we could ever give ourselves. This growing relationship with God is possible because he calls us and then enables us by his abundant grace and the Holy Spirit.

Our longing can be like Paul's: "I want to know Christ." God will answer this heart-cry with himself in ever-increasing fullness.

Anyone who has not yet responded to God's invitation for forgiveness and new birth into a new life can know him in saving grace. We who are already Christians by birth from above can know Christ as Paul desired to know him. We can know Christ intimately. We can know him in union with his will. We can know him more and more—in a deeper and deeper loving relationship in an ever-increasing fullness.

If Paul can want to know Christ in this way, so can we. James wrote, "*you do not have because you do not ask*" (James 4:2). Could we also say, "We do not have because we do not want, we do not hunger?"

It doesn't matter how much God has blessed us or how far we have advanced in our walk with him. There is always more of God to know.

We can have a more excellent experience of his love and a more marvelous manifested filling of his Spirit.

Each day can be a fresh start in our relationship with God, in this fellowship beyond description or measure in its wonder. Trials and difficulties are a part of this life. We will experience heartaches and sorrow. But our hearts can still overflow with the peace and joy of his presence and the surety of his promises. We can genuinely know Christ and then lovingly and powerfully show Christ to those around us.

This world's values are all mixed up, but we can know what matters most. We can say with Paul and all the other like-hearted saints through the ages, "I want to know Christ." I want to know Christ in intimate communion. I want to know Christ in union with his will, and I want to know Christ in ever-increasing fullness. We can be a blessed part of this amazing love story at the heart of the universe.

Chapter 4

The Greatest Love Story

Is there a purpose for the universe with its vast distances beyond comprehension, a universe filled with billions of galaxies, each with billions of stars? Why does it exist?

God created the universe for a specific, significant, and astonishing purpose. Ultimately, God's act of creation was to bring him glory. But why did God create the cosmos to bring him glory? The universe is an amazing work of creativity, precision, and astonishing beauty. However, there is something more than the manifold wisdom of God in all the beauty of created things. Beyond its natural wonder, there is a purpose for it all that is so profound and amazing that our small hearts and limited minds can hardly take it in.

God created the world to prepare for himself, for Christ, a bride. God has fashioned the universe in all its wonder and placed men and women on a small planet in the Milky Way Galaxy, so he could prepare a people with whom he could share his love and life for all of eternity. This act of love is the purpose of it all. Creation is for us to enjoy, but we were placed specifically in the world that we might choose to know and love and worship God and, by the act of his grace, glory in his presence now and forever. God brought forth the universe out of nothing so you and I could choose to know him intimately, and wonder of wonders, so he could lavish his love upon us.

David, realizing something of the wonder of it all, wrote these words, *"When I consider Your heavens, the work of Your fingers, the moon and the stars, which You have ordained, what is man that You are mindful of him, and the son of man that You visit him?"* (Ps. 8:3-4).

This truth is astounding. How can we ever begin to grasp the marvel of it? Christ wanted a bride. Beyond himself, God wanted a lover who, by a real choice, would love him passionately and forever. He made the world so you and I could be born and be part of a divine fellowship of love. The purpose of the universe is about a breathtaking, divine romance.

We long for love because God made us in the image of perfect love. He created us for our relationship with Christ. Nothing else will satisfy. Some movie studios have recognized, and have tried to capture, our longing for a fulfillment that fairy tales and romantic, magical adventures with happy endings demonstrate. This longing for romance and adventure, this longing to pursue what is worthwhile and lasting, this longing to be pursued, because we are of value, our Creator placed in our hearts. We can only be satisfied by a life lived in the ultimate, romantic adventure with God himself.

God doesn't need our love. God is complete in himself in the Trinity of the Father, Son, and Holy Spirit in an eternal fellowship and sharing of love. Love is not a chemical, hormonal event in our bodies or just a construct of our mind or imagination. Love is who God is. Divine love exists as the intimate communion and communication between the Father, Son, and Holy Spirit. This love flows within and among the Godhead for all eternity, and God is complete in that perfect love. He needs nothing. But in his boundless love, God has chosen to create us and invite us to share in the Holy Trinity's love. In the giving of his love and the receiving of ours, God is truly glorified.

The Song of Songs in our Bible is a romantic, even provocative, Oriental love poem. *"My lover spoke and said to me, 'Arise, come, my darling; my beautiful one, come with me'"* (Song of Sol. 2:10 NIV). In the literal sense, Song of Songs is a poem of ardent love between a husband and wife, between the lover and the beloved. But God meant this love poem to be an allegory that represents the fervent love between God and Israel; Christ and his bride, the church; and between Christ and each person who claims Christ as Savior, lover, and Lord of their lives. This love poem is in God's Word because this divine romance is the central truth and purpose of creation.

The need and longing of modern men and women are what the need and longing of the human race have always been: To find answers to the questions—"Who am I?" "Why am I here?" "Do I have value?" "What is my purpose?" "What matters in this life that I live?" In the reality of the beautiful divine romance, we find the answers to these existential questions. In this great love story, we find our own stories. In this divine romance, we discover and experience who we are, why we are here, and the reason and hope of our living. How can we get to the indescribable marvel, the unfathomable richness, and immense importance of what this sacred romance means for our lives now and eternity!

From the beginning of time, true history has been about this divine romance—about God reaching to embrace us in his love and fulfill us in his purposes. All that has happened, in the world and our individual lives, has been about this romance. It's been about God calling us to himself, his love, and his will. God's will for us ushers us into his present and future kingdom, where we experience fulfillment, and God is truly glorified.

When God placed Adam and Eve in the Garden of Eden, it was that he might love them, and they love him in return. When God called Abraham out of Ur of Chaldea, it was to invite him on an adventure of love, bring him to a land where a people could be God's beloved, and then be a demonstration and invitation to the world of God's love. When God delivered the children of Israel from Egypt, it was to bring them to a land he called Beulah Land, the "land of the married." God's desire and God's plan was for the people to be married to him. The law of the Old Covenant given on Mt. Sinai was a schoolmaster to point the children of Israel beyond the laws to the lover who was behind them. "Love me" was the call of God. Love me "*with all your heart, with all your soul, and with all your strength*" (Deut. 6:5). When God prescribed the tabernacle structure, he was in the holy of holies, a patient lover, longing for the time when the veil would be rent, and he could embrace his people in passionate, divine love. God sent prophets to sound out the call of a lover to his beloved and call Israel to turn from her other lovers.

The Old Testament story is one of God reaching for his bride. But time after time, God's love was rejected, and his people committed adultery with false gods. When it seemed there was nothing more he could do, then God came himself to win back his bride. God came to enable us to fulfill our glorious destiny in his love. Christ came to reveal on the cross of Calvary the measureless depth of his love and the wondrous scope of his purposes for his bride. There on the cross, God's heart was torn open in the greatest wound of love the universe has ever known. In his love, God took upon himself all the adulterous and idolatrous sins that separated us from the fellowship of his love. God did this so he could win his bride. He did it all in this great love story that is the reason for creation.

God removed the barriers to our intimate fellowship with him. God's continuous desire has been to embrace us in his divine love. God waited patiently behind the veil that separated us from his blazing love. I like to think that the sound of a mighty, rushing wind from heaven on that day of Pentecost was the sound of God rushing to embrace his beloved. This embrace of God was the purpose of creation and the desire of his heart all along.

The New Testament, also, is full of images, parables, and proclamations that reveal the relationship between Christ and the church as one of the bridegroom and bride in spiritual marriage. Paul wrote to the church of Ephesus, and he writes to each of us: *"Husbands, love your wives, just as Christ also loved the church and gave Himself for her, that he might sanctify and cleanse her with the washing of water by the word, that he might present her to Himself a glorious church, not having spot or wrinkle or any such thing, but that she should be holy and without blemish. 'For this reason a man shall leave his father and mother and be joined to his wife, and the two shall become one flesh.' This is a great mystery, but I speak concerning Christ and the church"* (Eph. 5:25-27, 31-32).

Why does God put so much emphasis on marriage and the relationship between a husband and wife? A long and healthy marriage holds great importance for the family and a nation. Marriage is the God-ordained, social institution that provides a stable foundation for society. When the institution of marriage is not functioning and stable as God intended, society is not properly functioning or stable. As marriages and the family go, so goes the world. For this reason, our understanding of the family as God designed and purposed is so essential. With all of this being true, we must further see that marriage has the grand purpose of picturing and pointing us to the relationship of love between God and his people, between Christ and his bride.

Do you think it was without purpose or heavenly significance that Jesus performed his first miracle at a wedding (John 2:1-11)? Jesus had come into the world to win his bride for the grandest, most important marriage of all time in the greatest romance story ever told. When he was celebrating with the bride and groom at the marriage supper, was he anticipating his own intimate relationship with his people who would be his forever? Was Jesus thinking of his own beautiful, beloved bride and the willing price he would pay at the cross to consummate this spiritual communion for an eternity of incomparable love? In Christ's heart, was he celebrating his forthcoming marriage with a joy that only true love could know? A yearning love for his own bride must surely have been his heart's experience that day as he performed a miracle that revealed that what comes by a miracle of grace always brings the best.

No wonder God declares that the greatest commandment is, " ... *You shall love the Lord your God with all your heart, with all your soul, and with all your mind"* (Matt. 22:37). This love is the fulfillment of the purpose of the universe. God is a righteously jealous God, for he knows that only when we love him supremely will we be supremely satisfied, and will God be supremely glorified.

To live for and live from this place of supreme love for God focuses and directs everything about our lives. The desire to please the One who loves us lavishly fills every moment. We want to spend time with our true love. Prayer becomes a sacred rendezvous, a longed-for, cherished place where we meet with the lover of our souls. Although we can commune with God throughout the day, we look forward to those intimate, chosen times with God in prayer. Our time of prayer becomes our oasis in the desert, our peace in the storm, our joy, our strength, and our place of receiving the supernatural life and divine love of God that we need and desire so desperately.

From the place of unreserved love for God, we read the Word of God with renewed freshness and excitement as a love letter from our lover. We cherish God's written word, but we also seek close fellowship with the loving God to which the inspired words point us. Every moment and action of our lives can become a willing offering to the One in whose love we are fulfilled. We follow God's commandments and obey his Holy

Spirit because we love him and because pleasing the One who has pursued us with his enduring love is our greatest joy.

The Bible tells us that we, whom God loved so much, caused a cataclysmic crisis in the universe. We were stolen by an enemy, with our consent, from our true husband and lover. What did God do? God carried out the most significant rescue warfare operation in the history of the world to win us back. God created us for a love relationship with him. When we turned away from him, he promised to come for us. The love story of the ages is about how God sought us to bring us home to himself. God sent blessings. He sent messengers with words of love and warning. When everything else failed, God put into action the most audacious, daring plan ever conceived. Under the concealment of night, the Creator of the world came into the enemy camp unrecognized with his identity veiled, hidden as a baby born in a manger. When the world was under the power of evil, God came to set us free from the fraudulent promises and malicious chains of a false lover. What did God see in us that caused him to act so dramatically, so adventurously? Why did he act like a jealous lover? Why did God come and deliver us from our blatant adultery at such a price to himself? He did it because of his immeasurable, inexhaustible, ever-unfolding, never failing, self-sacrificing love. God came for us, and he reaches for us still despite our unfaithfulness.

In one of the classics of literature, the *Iliad*, Homer relates the story of the Trojan War. Men fought this ancient war over a beautiful woman named Helen. Helen must have been extraordinary. People said of her that "she had a face that launched a thousand ships." Helen was the wife of Menelaus, king of Sparta of Greece. Paris, prince of Troy, visited the Grecian kingdom and wanted Helen as his own. Paris slipped away with Helen and took her back to Troy. The king of Greece so valued Helen that he set sail for Troy with 1,000 ships and a mighty army to win Helen back. Few women may have ever felt so pursued as Helen.

God so valued us that he launched heaven's best to pursue us and win us back. To think that God would so treasure us, that he would pursue us with such an astonishing reach of love is marvelous beyond our understanding! Here is the greatest romance story the world has ever known! Here is a love story older than the story of Helen and the Trojan

War. God had us on his mind before the foundation of the world and loved us before time began.

God is still reaching for his bride, for each of us, to offer us the full fellowship of his love. He is seeking each of us. He is pursuing his bride. How can we not say yes to such a love? How can we not give our hearts without reservation to such a God?

Someday Jesus is coming back. Why is he coming again? He is coming for his bride. What a glorious day that will be when Jesus comes to receive us who have given our bridal love to him, to the One who pursued us in love and purchased us with the price of his blood.

Jesus was the sacrificial Lamb of God slain for atonement for our sins. This present world will have ended, and the new age will have begun with the marriage supper of the Lamb. *"Let us be glad and rejoice and give Him glory, for the marriage of the Lamb has come, and His wife has made herself ready"* (Rev. 19:7). *" ... Blessed are those who are called to the marriage supper of the Lamb!"* (Rev. 19:9). The marriage supper of the Lamb, this feast of love that brings us to our divine lover's very presence, is the culmination of present-day history and, yet, is just the beginning of a love story that will last forever, ages without end.

So Longs My Soul

So Longs My Soul

So Longs My Soul

So Longs My Soul

So Longs My Soul

Chapter 5

The "Oh" at the Heart of True Religion

"Oh, that You would rend the heavens! That You would come down! That the mountains might shake at Your presence—as fire burns brushwood, as fire causes water to boil—to make Your name known" (Isa. 64:1-2).

When we consider a portion of God's Word to study for understanding and application, we might choose an entire book of the Bible. We would seek to learn what it meant for those to whom it was first written and what it means for us today. Or, we could choose a chapter of the Bible or maybe only a few verses. Sometimes we might select just one verse or occasionally just one exceptionally fruitful phrase and then seek God's heart from his inspired words.

Let's study not the whole book of Isaiah, not one chapter, not a few verses, not even one verse, not even one phrase. Let us consider just one word—the word "Oh." I am not trying to do something "cute" or "flippant" with the sacred Word of God, nor am I trying to play some kind of homiletical game with the text. However, this word "Oh" catches the prophet's passion and unveils the heart of his message as he cries out to God for the people and the work of God.

I like stories about commitment—stories in which people show a passion for what they do, like athletes who have committed themselves to be their very best. I excite over accounts of artists, or entrepreneurs, or soldiers, or teachers or others who give themselves in dedication to be outstanding in their fields of endeavor. I especially like stories of men and women who have a great passion for God—people like David, Mary of Magdalen, and the Apostle Paul. I am also deeply inspired by men and women who lived after the Bible times whose hearts have been aflame with love for Christ; people who were moved to utter commitment and passionate, reverent obedience to God. If anything is worthy of passionate devotion, it is our Jesus, his way, and his kingdom.

In chapter sixty-three of Isaiah, the prophet laments that God seems so far from his people. In chapter sixty-four, Isaiah calls on God to come to their aid. Throughout the book of Isaiah, the reason for this called-for intervention of God is that the nations may know his name. Only when the world sees God blessing and defending a transformed people will they recognize who God is.

So, Isaiah cries out: "Oh, God that you would rend the heavens and come down!" in miraculous power as in the past. This "Oh" of Isaiah's intercessory cry is at the very heart of true religion. This "Oh" is the very heartthrob of our walk with God. This word appears throughout Scripture, sometimes as "Oh," other times as "O." It is not always the same word in the original Hebrew. Sometimes the term is arrived at by a combination of words. The expression is used as an exclamation and used with the meaning of incitement. It can preface words of petition, love, or praise. The "Oh" adds passion or fervency or the sigh of longing to words that follow.

In some translations, we do not see the word "Oh" in a few verses because of how the expression combines with other words in Hebrew. Many of the most literal translations will give the "Oh" because it accurately expresses the intent of God's Word to convey desire and intense longing. So, we find Jeremiah crying out, *"Oh, that my head were waters, and my eyes a fountain of tears, that I might weep day and night for the slain of the daughter of my people!"* (Jer. 9:1), and David prays, *"Hear, O Lord, when I cry with my voice!"* (Ps. 27:7).

"Oh" expresses awe, concern, passion, or ardent longing. What is sad and significant is that the "Oh" has gone out of religion for many. The "Oh" is not a part of their faith experience of God. This "Oh" in the heart is the difference between nominal and authentic Christianity. Without this "Oh" inspired by the Holy Spirit, we have dead orthodoxy. It's the "Oh" we need in our faith. It's our heart-cry to God, our cry of passion for God and his work.

This "Oh" is not an expression of mere emotion, though emotion is an integral part of who we are as creatures of God in his image. Without emotion in our relationship with God, we do not have real or full worship. This "Oh" is a living, fearsome, whole-person response to God himself and to his love and grace offered us through the work of Calvary. This "Oh" is a zealous devotion and a stirring of soul and spirit that moves us to worship and witness. This "Oh" in the soul is born of God but made ours by our choice to respond to him.

We need this "Oh" in our religion, our faith, our walk with God. This "Oh" in our souls is crucial if we are to experience all God has for us, and if we are to carry out God's purposes to glorify his name. In what ways do we need this "Oh"?

We need the "Oh" in our repentance. Our repentance can be shallow for just relief from our guilt, but this is no real repentance. We can only make it a matter of "accepting Christ" as if he is privileged to be allowed into our living. We should have real sorrow for our sin and rebellion and turn to God as a beggar, desperate in our need of him. We turn from our past, receive his promised grace, and then walk with God in the way of his love and holiness. In the Hebrides revival, the renowned but humble preacher, Duncan Campbell, had to stop preaching at times because he couldn't be heard over the people crying out loudly in sorrow for their sins.

Even as Christians, we can take our sins lightly. John the Apostle wrote to Christians, *"If we confess our sins, He is faithful and just to forgive us our sins and to cleanse us from all unrighteousness"* (1 John 1:9). True repentance is the secret of victory, joy, and power in our Christian lives. If there were more "Oh" in our repentance, there would be more victory in our walk. We need an "Oh" in our repentance.

We need an "Oh" in our praise and worship. More than something passionless, our personal and group worship should be full of heartfelt, grateful exuberance or expressed in sublime but powerful silence in God's overwhelming presence. True worship with music is not about musical style. It's about the "Oh" in the soul. If there is passionate, extravagant worship, God will manifest his presence. God is everywhere present. He is personally present with every Christian by his Holy Spirit, but we need his manifested presence. God will reveal his presence when his people genuinely worship him. He inhabits, he "is enthroned in" the praises of his people (Ps. 22:3). We need "Oh" in our praise and worship.

We need an "Oh" in our reverent, awestruck response to the wonder of God—the wonder of who he is, what he's done, and what he offers. We need an "Oh" in response to what we know of his attributes of holiness, love, justice, faithfulness, wisdom, and power. We need to be in awe over the mystery of the unknowable depths of God's glory, and over to the beauty and wonders of creation. We need an "Oh" in our response to the marvel of the incarnation and Calvary and Christ's resurrection and ascension to heaven to rule his kingdom and intercede for us at the Father's right hand. " ... *Who is like you—majestic in holiness, awesome in glory, working wonders?"* (Exod. 15:11 NIV). We need this "Oh" in our response to the wonder of who God is and who he is for us.

We need an "Oh" in our love for God as our response to God's love for us. How can our hearts take in the matchless, measureless love of God? When we truly experience his love, we are overwhelmed. We are wholly ravished! How can we express our wonder, our joy? Our heart's response must be like King David's, *"I will love You, O Lord, my strength"* (Ps. 18:1).

God's love was poured out at Calvary for the world, for each of us, for me. Some people thought that I was beyond God's reach, that I had gone too far in my rebellion and rejection of God. But God's grace broke into my life, and God embraced me in his love. My life has never been the same and has never been a more exciting, joyous adventure. "*But God demonstrates His own love toward us, in that while we were still sinners* (when we were his enemies), *Christ died for us"* (Rom. 5:8). Our response should be a passionate love for him—love like a fire within us—raging, radical, extravagant, and blazing. We respond to God with a love that opens our hearts to all he is and all he has done for us—love that calls us to give ourselves entirely to him in trust and obedience.

This love is not a sentimental, soft love but a tough, tested, tenacious, triumphant love that will take us through any trial. Lack of the "Oh," lukewarmness, could be one of the greatest sins of Christians and the church. Lukewarmness is abhorrent to God. " ... *Because you are lukewarm, and neither cold nor hot, I will vomit you out of My mouth"* (Rev. 3:16).

We need real, exciting, adventurous romance in our faith, in our love relationship with God. This love story is what the universe is all about. God created us for this astounding divine romance. There should be in our relationship with God real romance, just like an "Oh" should be in our marriage relationship with our spouse. I have been married to my wife for more than forty-seven years, yet when I see my wife enter a room or hear her voice on the phone, my heart still throbs in genuine excitement. How much more should this breathtaking, passionate love be in our relationship with God! We need an "Oh" in our love for God in our response to his love.

We need an "Oh" in our hunger for God himself—in our longing for him, his work, and his glory. *"As the deer pants for the water brooks, so pants my soul for You, O God"* (Ps. 42:1). *"O God, you are my God, earnestly I seek you; my soul thirsts for you"* (Ps. 63:1 NIV). There is so much in our fallen world to stifle our hunger for Christ. We want to look for ways to stir up that hunger and avoid what takes it away. We need an "Oh" in our longing for God, and God will answer with himself.

We need an "Oh" in how we view the people of this world who are living without God in their lives. We need a passion for the lost. Where is the "Oh" of heart-broken anguish and weeping when so many are living and dying without God? Millions of people in this world and people right around us are missing eternal life in Christ. Paul was in Athens, where there were grand monuments and spectacular buildings, including the Acropolis with the imposing Parthenon. These architectural wonders did not move Paul. He didn't even mention them, but we read that *"his spirit was stirred in him, when he saw the city wholly given to idolatry"* (Acts 17:16 AV). There was an "Oh" in his heart. We need an "Oh" in our hearts for the lost.

We need an "Oh" in our love for God's church. Jesus *"loved the church and gave Himself for her"* (Eph. 5:25). Jesus came into the world to call to himself a people, a bride forever. If Jesus so loves the church, so should we. We should love the church, pray for her, live for her, die for her that she might be a bride prepared. Yet, our hearts should break that the church has missed much of God's blessing and supernatural power and has had such little impact on the world. We can spend more time and energy fighting among ourselves in the church than we do lifting Jesus to the world. Oh, that the church might genuinely be in spiritual oneness for the sake of God's purposes and glory! Paul wrote: *"My dear children, for whom I am again in the pains of childbirth until Christ is formed in you"* (Gal. 4:19 NIV). We need an "Oh" in our cry for the church.

We need an "Oh" in our praying. We need prayers from the heart, prayers that stand on the promises of God's Word, and prayers inspired and anointed by the Holy Spirit. In his sovereignty, love, and superabundant grace, God has chosen to work through his people's prayers. God waits for us to pray, but how often does he wait in vain? The need is not for complacent prayers, not for selfish, passionless, or powerless prayers. Nor does God need fancy, showy prayers. God waits for simple, childlike, trusting prayers; fervent and expectant prayers; prayers prayed from a stirred heart; prayers that cry out with an "Oh" of longing and bring God to work wonders in this world. The need is great in this world for God to manifest his presence and his work. God has promised to answer if we pray. We need an "Oh" in our praying. Let's pray. Let's pray passionately. Let's see God do his work.

We need an "Oh" in our longing for revival—for a mighty, supernatural work of God's grace and power. Great but humble men and women of God have longed for God's mighty work in times of great need, knowing that a real move of God was the only hope and answer. In the passage of God's Word in which we have considered this, "Oh," Isaiah sees the necessity of his times and cries out, *"Oh, that You would rend the heavens! That You would come down! That the mountains might shake at Your presence—as fire burns brushwood, as fire causes water to boil— to make Your name known"* (Isa. 64:1-2). We need some mountains to shake, some heavenly fire to fall, some water to boil! We need God to work. We need an "Oh" in our longing for revival. One of the reasons we have not had a revival and great spiritual awakening in this world, our nation, our churches, and our lives is that we have been content to live without it. We need an "Oh" in our longing and living for revival.

We need an "Oh" in our watching for his return. This present world is not our home. We, who are his children by birth from above, will live with God eternally. The One who gave himself for us is returning to receive us to himself. If we love him, then we yearn to see his face and be with him forever. We want to live with hearts made pure and prepared until he comes.

We need an "Oh" in our desire for God to be glorified. This "Oh" to glorify God should be our greatest desire. All the other ways in which an "Oh" is vital in our religion are so God will be glorified. God is so little honored, and yet he is so supremely worthy. We need an "Oh" in our desire to glorify God in our lives, his church, and the nations.

We need an "Oh" in our daily, confident expectation of what God is going to do. We need faith that is trust-filled, joyful anticipation of God's miraculous work for ourselves, those we love, the church, and the world. We need an "Oh" in our hearts each morning as we rise, knowing there is an adventure before us in God's love. We need an "Oh" in our daily walk with God.

We can have this exclamation in our soul. This "Oh" is the heart of our love for God, the fountain of our worship, and the breath of our trust. We have propositional truth given by God's revelation in his Word by which we measure and evaluate all things, but this Word calls for our response in love to our God himself, the person at the center of our faith.

Every person is different. Everyone will express passion differently through each of their unique personalities. But we must all have an "Oh." We must all have an "Oh" by which we take up our cross and offer obedience. More than emotion, it is a choice of love, a response to God's love, God's Word, and God's call. This "Oh" is our response to God that reaches for satisfaction in him alone.

Yet, there is something more, something so marvelous that we can hardly grasp it. This "Oh" first begins with God. The "Oh" is in his heart! God's heart is a great, passionate, perfect exclamation of love.

Before the creation of the world, the "Oh" was in God's heart, in his thoughts and plans for his bride, the church, and for each of us. This "Oh" was God's at creation, when " ... *God saw everything that He made, and indeed it was very good"* (Gen. 1:31). This "Oh" was in God's heart for the children of Israel. *"Oh, that they had such a heart in them that they would fear Me and always keep all My commandments, that it might be well with them and with their children forever!"* (Deut. 5:29). Jesus came to us in the incarnation with an "Oh" from God's heart that we might respond to his reach of love. At Calvary, there was an "Oh" of love expressed by God that was great enough to embrace all of fallen humanity. At the resurrection, God proclaimed a triumphant "Oh" that would overcome every plan of Satan and redirect the eternal destiny of his people and the world. At Pentecost, what God had desired and planned all along came to pass with a world-changing "Oh" as Christ embraced his bride in the Holy Spirit with the sound as a mighty rushing wind.

There will be an "Oh" in God's heart at his return "Oh, my bride! My bride!" In heaven, not only will we be thrilled with God, but God will be thrilled with us. A magnificent and holy "Oh" of God will fill heaven forever. The reward of those who commit to the things of this world does not compare to the blessing and eternal reward of those whose passionate commitment is first to God and his purposes.

To this very day, God has an "Oh" of longing for each of us personally. He longs that we would know him intimately, love him supremely, and step into his plan and blessing. Our God has this heart for us. He inspires this exclamation, this "Oh," in our souls. Now we can inspire this holy and ardent aspiration in one another.

Do we have this "Oh"—this passion—in our lives for God, his will, his work, and his glory? We must not be satisfied until we are satisfied. Sometimes when we have been on this journey for a while with Jesus, we could lose the wonder, passion, this "Oh" in our souls. This loss of devotion can be because of trials, adversity, negligence, or slothfulness. We must not let this happen. God is worthy of our passionate love. The need in this world is enormous. Jesus is coming soon. May the fire of our love and devotion grow even stronger that we may be the hands and the feet and the burning heart that bring this consuming fire of God's love to the world. May there be an "Oh" at the heart of our relationship with God.

Chapter 6

Rahab's Real Romance

The book of Joshua is a great adventure story. I love it. It describes how God tries to help his people, the children of Israel, claim the promises he has given them—promises to claim a land, be a nation, and have a special relationship with God. As they would live in that promise, they would be a demonstration of what God would be to a people who will trust him.

After wandering for forty years, the children of Israel again have gotten to the edge of the land of promise. Joshua sends out spies to look over the territory, especially the mighty, walled city of Jericho. We read the story in Joshua 2:1-24; 6:20-25. And where do these spies go? Get this now. The spies go to the house of a prostitute—yes, a harlot, as Joshua calls her. They go to the home of Rahab.

Why would these spies go to the house of a prostitute? They did not go for immoral purposes. There were several good reasons why the spies would go to Rahab's house. For one thing, they might get easily lost here, concealed among the people coming and going. For another reason, it was probably a credible place to get information. But primarily, I believe God saw an honest and hungry heart that needed deliverance and would respond to his grace.

God is always looking for someone to respond to his love. Where will he find that person? In the house of a prostitute? I am not promoting prostitution—but who is beyond God's reach? For many of us, God had to make a long reach to bring us to himself.

There is something else important here. I believe the spies had pure hearts and real faith. In Joshua 2:14, we read that the spies said to Rahab, *"when the Lord has given us the land"*—not "if," but "when." The spies believed God's promises. The city of Jericho had massive, impenetrable walls and was a literal fortress. These spies still believed God, in contrast to the ten spies the first time the Israelites approached to enter Canaan.

What is Rahab's perspective of all of this? She is a harlot in a heathen land. The Canaanites had horrible, polluted worship filled with perverted sex practices. Rahab felt trapped with no way out. But something begins to happen to her. She hears of a nation that trusts in one God. She learns what the Hebrew God has done for them. He parted the Red Sea. He led them with a pillar of fire and defeated their enemies. She surely knows something about the corruption of man. She knows that this is not right— that there must surely be something better. Rahab begins to wonder: "What could a God like that do for me?" She has longed for something more, something better for her life.

Then, something happens. Rahab encounters two men of God. One day two men that are different come to her house. She knows it right away. She knows it by the way they look at her and the way that they speak to her. There's a glow on their faces and a sparkle in their eyes that is not the fire of lust but the passion for the glory of a holy God. In her heart, she wonders, "What is this I sense?" Instead of taking her body, they share their God. Hope springs up in her heart.

The most beautiful thing takes place. Rahab believes! Amid a heathen world, she believes! In the middle of a pagan and evil culture, she chooses to believe.

God can reach us anywhere. Rahab had a choice, and she chose to believe. This Canaanite believed and passed from the kingdom of Canaanites to the kingdom of God. More than change nations, she changed kingdoms. Isn't it a great story!

The book of Hebrews makes a tremendous statement about Rahab. It counts her among the heroes of the faith. *"By faith the harlot Rahab did not perish with those who did not believe, when she had received the spies with peace"* (Heb. 11:31). God's Word listed her with Abraham, Jacob, Joseph, and Moses—great heroes of the faith.

How was it that Rahab was spared destruction with the rest of the city? How was she given a promise for a new start, a new home and a new nation? Rahab had hidden the spies so that the men of Jericho could not find them, and then she helped the spies escape through a window in the city wall. Rahab had a desperate request. *" … I beg you, swear to me by the Lord, since I have shown you kindness, that you also will show kindness to my father's house"* (Josh. 2:12). The spies promised that they would spare her. They told her to identify her home by binding a scarlet cord in the window so the Israelite army would not destroy her and her family. The spies escaped, and Rahab hung the scarlet marker out of her window so the children of Israel would know that she trusted in God, and they would spare her life and the life of her family.

Imagine Rahab's excitement and her hope as she put out the cord. Could this be happening to her? Her life had seemed hopeless and in ruins. Now there was hope for a change in her life and for her family to be saved when the city fell. Imagine her rushing out and gathering up her family. "My life has changed! There's hope for me, hope for us!" "Come with me to my house." And she persuaded them! Do we have enough conviction, enough excitement, enough fire in our hope to convince anyone?

Consider the courage of Rahab. If the king of Jericho found out what Rahab had done, she would suffer a cruel death. She had to remain in a Canaanite kingdom between the time she declared allegiance to the living God, and the time judgment fell on the city. This trust in God's faithfulness took courage.

But think with me. This trust is how a Christian lives as a pilgrim in this world in an alien culture, controlled by Satan. We need the courage to hold to our faith in God's promises. Rahab believed. Rahab put out the scarlet cord.

You know the next part of the story. God gave Israel a supernatural victory over the city of Jericho as those strong walls came tumbling down. The Israeli soldiers found the home with the scarlet cord at its window. *"And the young men who had been spies went in and brought out Rahab, her father, her mother, her brothers, and all that she had"* (Josh. 6:23). The same spies she had saved caught her away and delivered her and her family. What deliverance! What a story!

But there's more! A tradition says that Rahab married one of the spies, one of those she helped and then came to her rescue. I wonder if she had any idea that when these pure men first visited her, one of them would marry her. What a great story! But there's more!

Scripture tells us the name of the young Israelite that she married. His name was Salmon, son of Nahshon. Who was Nahshon? According to Scripture, Nahshon was—now get this, I love it—Nahshon was a great prince of the tribe of Judah (1 Chron. 2:10-11 AV). Salmon was of a princely family. This story is amazing! It is wildly exciting! The harlot who became a believer became the wife of a prince, a prince of Judah!

Talk about being carried away by a prince! What an adventure! What a story of romance! There's still more!

Christ came into the world from Rahab's family line! On the human side, Rahab was an ancestor of King David and eventually of the Messiah himself. Rahab was the great, (thirty-two times) grandmother of Jesus (Matt. 1:4-6). This story has really gotten good! Rahab, the harlot, believes, is carried away by a prince who marries her, and she becomes the ancestor of Jesus Christ. What a story!

Do we know that we find ourselves in Rahab's place? All of us are worthy of judgment, but we, like Rahab, can choose to believe God. We can believe as Rahab in the midst of a wicked world, and God will deliver us to a new kingdom. We can become sons and daughters of the Creator, children of the King. We can become part of a great adventure, a great romance, the story of all stories.

How? How can we be brought to such an undeserved but privileged place? We, too, have a scarlet cord—the blood of Christ. Jesus shed his real blood on the cross for us. He came to rescue us when we were without hope in this world, and the walls were falling. When we trust in his shed blood on Calvary as an atoning sacrifice for our forgiveness, for deliverance, and reconciliation to our heavenly Father, God brings us into a whole new kingdom with a whole new level of living.

This scarlet cord runs all through the Bible. It is the theme of all real history if we only could see it. This sacred, sacrificial provision was on the heart of God before the creation of the world. This scarlet cord was in the stories of Adam and Eve, Noah, Abraham, the deliverance of the children of Israel from Egypt, the Passover, the crossing of the Jordan River, and the temple sacrifices. All these point us to Christ, to the Lamb slain who was our entrance into the divine romance, the greatest love story of all times.

The scarlet cord is out the window of people's lives who trust God's grace for forgiveness, deliverance, and a born-from-above new life. Today this is our hope. What do we have hanging out the windows of our lives? People try all kinds of things. Only the scarlet cord will save us— only this is the sign of our faith in the saving work of Christ and our allegiance to God.

Jesus will be returning. He will come as savior, judge, deliverer, and as a groom for his bride. Then the walls of this present world will come tumbling down. What will matter when he comes? Our material possessions? Our good looks? Our earthly position and power? Our educational degrees? The acclaim of men? The only thing that will matter is that we are under the promise and protection of the scarlet cord, showing that we believe and love the One who saves us by his mercy.

Christ's sacred blood has never lost its power to save and deliver us. This blood is our plea. We have none other. The scarlet cord, the blood of Christ, is our plea for forgiveness, deliverance, protection, healing, access to God and Christ's resurrection power, and God's gift of the Holy Spirit.

Some may respond, "You do us a disservice when you speak of a hero prince and romance and miraculous deliverances. Life is not like that." Listen, I know, for sure, that there are heartaches, struggles, and difficulties in this life. I have experienced some severe trials myself. Because we are excited about the adventure of the kingdom of God doesn't mean we won't have hardships, but it does mean that we see the big picture and the larger hope. Without adversity, we have no adventure. Rahab had difficulties, but she still had adventure and romance. Rahab fulfilled her destiny. So can we.

I will not be impressed with cynical dream bashers. By God's help, I will not be moved, deterred, or turned aside by faith-squashers or God doubters. Although situations and relationships may disappoint us in this world, God will never disappoint us or fail in his promises. What you look at determines what you see. I want to see Jesus. If I look at Jesus first, I will see everything else differently.

Why is it some see romance when others see only adversity? We observe people in the same circumstance, the same kind of difficulties, yet one person sees adventure while another sees only reversals and disasters. What will we see? Rahab saw by faith her deliverance and a new life. She put her life on the line for what she saw. We can see Christ and what he has done for us. We can hang the crimson cord out the window of our lives. This truth is not a fairy tale. Whatever we face in this world, if we let Christ be our prince, our Lord, and our deliverer, the end ultimately will be a happy ever after.

We must realize that there is no romance without commitment—in our marriages or our Christian lives. I have never met a fully committed Christian who didn't find a walk with God to be a joyful adventure. Adversity? Yes. Times of terrible distress? Yes. But in light of eternity, a venture that is worth it all.

If we are not living in the freedom or the fullness of real life and realize we are in a doomed city, we can put out a scarlet cord and begin the romance. If we are not living in a real adventure, here's what we can do. We can commit ourselves fully to God and his adventure. This commitment is "THE" romance. Real romance is in proportion to real commitment.

We find hope in Rahab's real romance for the greatest love story. God is seeking his bride, and he is pursuing each of us in love. This adventure, this romance is God's story and our story. Everything in this world is about this epic tale of love. This love story is why our universe exists, and why we are in it. This adventure, this romance surpasses every other reality and every other human ambition in importance and implication for our living—this is our real romance.

If in days to come when someone writes our story, will it record that we believed God and that he delivered us to a new and fulfilled life like Rahab, or will it be just another crumbled wall story?

We can believe and put out the scarlet cord. We can commit ourselves to God and experience true romance and adventure. For this relationship with God, we can thirst. This blessing is ours to have in Christ to the glory of his name.

Chapter 7

My Love Story

"Come and hear, all you who fear God, and I will declare what He has done for my soul." Psalm 66:16

Everyone has a story. Each person has a personal narrative of how they live out their lives. What if people knew that their stories could be a part of a larger epic story with a grand purpose and eternal meaning? It could make a difference in how they evaluate life, other people, themselves and their choices, and even their eternal destiny.

God is reaching for each one of us to be a part of his amazing story. God sought after me when I didn't deserve it. When I had rejected him and fought against Christianity and the church and all that I thought they represented, God pursued me to make me a part of his amazing love story.

My parents raised me in a loving Christian home, but I always had a lot of questions, and I didn't think I was getting satisfactory answers. Throughout my public school education, I had good teachers, many of whom were probably Christians. However, in all the knowledge I was absorbing, my teachers made no mention of God and his part in any information I was receiving. The absence of the recognition of God in my studies was teaching me something. I wrongly began to think that God must not be necessary for the explanations of reality. At an early age, I was interested in the natural sciences and philosophy, always seeking answers. When I attended college, I majored in physics and mathematics and thought I had gotten some explanations for the way things are. However, physics and math didn't give all the answers and didn't seem immediately relevant concerning our human condition, so I then majored in sociology and philosophy. I eventually came to the wrong conclusion that there was no God. I became an avowed atheist. I believed that only the material universe existed and that scientific laws were adequate to account for all phenomena. I thought that the church was one of the greatest hindrances to human progress, because if there is no God, then religion is just a monumental waste of time, energy, and resources. I became involved in radical, campus politics. I was pushing for a non-violent revolution that would restructure society in such a way to ensure the survival of the species and still give individuals at least some degree of security and allow some personal pleasure and fulfillment. My definition of love? Love is an internal, chemical reaction and hormonal occurrence that is associated with certain external stimuli. Really warms you up, doesn't it?

But this view that I said I held of a godless universe did not satisfy. The answer left me empty. Honestly considered, such a belief could only lead to existential despair. There could be no real hope, authentic value, or meaning for my life. I had explained myself away. I was only a part of a cosmic machine and, in the end, had no more value or meaning than a tadpole. I just had a larger brain.

On one occasion, I vividly remember sitting beside a beautiful pond in pastureland on my grandfather's farm. The grasses around me were waving gently in the light breeze. A few small, fluffy clouds were floating across a blue sky. A few dozen yards to my right, a grove of pine trees lifted their branches to the sky. The evening sun was soon to set, and a reflection of the crimson orb in the pond water before me seemed as if it were pointing at me. It was breathtakingly beautiful. And yet, it was all meaningless. If there was no God, as I believed, it was all by chance and was purposeless. The incongruity of it all was truly perplexing. My only consolation was that I was honest in my despair.

My parents and others were praying for me. Many felt that I was beyond reach in my denial of God and my hostility to the church.

But one momentous day, a young man visited me at college. Howard had little advanced education at that time. He had been a rough street fighter. Howard told me how God had come into his heart and changed his life. He was radiant with joy and wept with tears of passionate love for God. I remember telling him, "I wish I could believe that, but I can't believe that any more than I can believe in a fairy tale." My words didn't faze him. He said, "Would you come with me? I'd like for you to meet some people." In a surprise to myself, I said I would. It was to be a heart-changing, life-changing experience.

I met a group of people who had genuine and exuberant joy and unfaked, amazing love for one another. It was something I couldn't explain away with my scientific, sociological, and philosophical interpretations. I realized, to be honest, I would have to reconsider this Christianity.

Then I was introduced to the writings of Dr. Francis Schaeffer. He described humankind's search through history for truth in science, philosophy, and the arts—a search of trying to find some universal, unifying truth that would make sense of all the particulars of our existence. His description of the historical search for truth described my search. Schaeffer helped to bring me to the honest conclusion that Christianity is intellectually acceptable. But something more was taking place. God was answering the prayers of my parents and others. He was calling me to himself.

I went to a church service as a part of my honest seeking. As it turned out, it happened to be a building fund, business meeting night. It didn't matter because that same genuine joy and love were in the worship in that place. I remember the people were singing about the happiness they had found in knowing and serving their Savior. I knew none of this joy. So I prayed a prayer.

How was I to pray? I hadn't believed in sin. There were only social norms that one could follow or not. The Bible had meant no more to me than a magazine or a comic book. But I wanted what was real. I wanted what was authentic. So I prayed the only way I could. "God, I don't know if you are real or not. But I want what's real. God, if you are real, get a hold of my life. Let me know. I want what's real!" And the tears flowed like rivers as I released the hunger of my heart.

Suddenly, I was filled with overwhelming, inexpressible love, cascading over me and coursing through me in a mighty torrent. I wasn't expecting this. I hadn't known what to expect. My scientific, mechanistic definition of love did not explain this experience. This love was true love—God's amazing love.

In the following days, as I began to read the Bible, God showed me that I was guilty of going my own way and not his way. God showed me the price paid by Christ to reconcile me to him and bring me home to his loving embrace.

I went back to that same field where I had felt such cosmic loneliness and despair earlier. Lifting my hands to God, I committed my life to him. I remember trying to sing part of a Christian song I had heard as a child. I'm not sure I got the words right, but I know God received them.

"Since Jesus gave His life for me, should I not give him mine. I'm consecrated Lord to Thee. I shall be wholly Thine. My all, O Lord, to Thee I give, accept it as Thine own; For Thee alone I'll ever live. My heart shall be Thy throne. My life, O Lord, I give to Thee, my talents, time, and all. I'll serve Thee Lord and faithful be. I'll hear Thy faintest call" (Mildred E. Howard, 1907-1993).

Heaven burst through upon me in a flood of divine love and joy. I knew without a doubt that this was the most real thing I had ever experienced. The scene around me—the tranquil pond, the grove of pine trees, the flowing sea of grass of the field, the blue sky with it floating clouds, the brilliant sun shining down upon it all now took on a whole new, breathtaking beauty and meaning. No longer was it purposeless and pointing me to despair. My heavenly Father had created it for my joy and his glory. Now I was his, and he was mine. The fields, the trees, the sky, the breeze were all raising praise to their creator. I joined them. I jumped, I ran, I danced through the field! I waved my arms and lifted my voice in praise to my God, my Redeemer!

I can't express the depths of my joy. This fellowship with God was the most exciting discovery of my life. There was an infinite and yet personal God. He loved me with unfathomable love, and I could know him personally. Nothing could surpass this in importance or wonder. This reality changed everything. I wanted to plunge into the depths of the ocean of God's love. God was more worthy of commitment than the shallow, revolutionary political ideas I once had. I wanted to give myself totally to this, with all the devotion of my heart. I began the most exciting adventure anyone could ever know—a walk with God with wonder and joy and eternal meaning. I was lost, but now I was found.

One of my earliest childhood memories was when I followed my dad's hunting dog out of our yard and into the woods. I remember losing sight of the dog and falling down a steep embankment into a ravine. I tried to climb back up the steep hill, but I couldn't make it. The evening was approaching, and it was getting dark. I became frightened. I began to cry out, "Daddy, Daddy, help me!" I still remember the sight of my dad appearing at the top of the hill. He climbed down, picked me up, put me on his shoulders, and carried me out of the woods. Daddy had found me, and I was going home! That day years later, in the field under the open blue sky, my heavenly Father found me and took me home. For the person responding to God, coming to God is like coming home. By God's grace, I have not lost the excitement or the sense of wonder of the all-encompassing answer of who God is and who he is for me in Christ.

Nothing compares to this. I once had lived in a world without God. Now I had met him, a loving God, at the center of all things. I had reason to be excited. God has forgiven me much, so I must love much. My story became a part of God's story—the most beautiful love story the world has ever known.

I have taken as my life's purpose to glorify God by being utterly and passionately given to this divine romance. I will experience this amazing love story in fullness as I live to know and love God intimately in Christ, and as I seek to honor him by doing his will and revealing his love in the power of his Spirit. This romance is possible only because of the marvelous, matchless, measureless work of God's grace. May God ever be praised and adored!

The French philosopher and mathematician, Descartes, once wrote: "I shall be entitled to entertain the highest expectations, if I am fortunate enough to discover only one thing that is certain and indubitable." By God's amazing grace, I have found that one thing that is certain and indubitable. God and his sacrificial love are at the heart of reality. An unchanging person and unfailing love are at the center of everything, and by this, we can measure all things and value all persons. Nothing could be more significant or wondrous.

Although everyone's personal story may not have such a dramatic conversion as mine, the truth is that every one of us has been separated from God by Adamic inheritance and by our own choices. God's great saving work of grace for each of us is worthy of genuine excitement, abundant joy, exuberant praise, and the passionate, total offering of ourselves to him.

My life, my dreams, my desires dramatically changed. I used my math and science training to teach school that year of my salvation. The following summer, I went to the church building, found an empty room down the hall from the main office, and told the pastor I would be there through the summer reading and praying. I asked him just to let me know if there was any way I could help him or serve the church in any way. God had gloriously changed the direction of my life, and I desired to serve him with the full devotion of my heart. I wanted to be a part of bringing God's love to this world in any way he might choose. That's how my ministry of service began. The one who was determined to do away with churches because he thought they were useless became a minister to proclaim Christ through the church as the only answer for the world. Surely God must have a sense of humor.

With such a change in my life, there was a radical change in the kind of woman I wanted to marry and with whom I could share this life of Christ. I knew my choice for a marriage partner was important. I now wanted a wife who would understand my new heart, a woman who would gladly choose to walk with me on this great adventure of grace.

A few months after my conversion, I traveled to a church meeting in Michigan and heard a special servant of God describe a close walk with God. In a few minutes, I was to my feet, exclaiming, "This is it! This is it!" This relationship with God was what my heart had longed for all along.

While I was seated there in the auditorium, I saw just the back of the head of the young lady sitting several rows in front of me. She had beautiful blonde hair that fell in ringlets over her shoulders. My heart jumped within me. I wasn't sure what was happening. I didn't know then all that God had in mind. I saw her again after the service. I don't believe we spoke to one another. I didn't even know her name, but I began to pray, "Lord, I don't know what this is you are trying to tell me, but if there is something here of your will for my life, you'll have to work it out. I don't even know how to contact her." (I thought she lived in Michigan but found out later she lived in Indiana.) "Lord, if you are in this you will have to bring her here to my church" (a small church in a distant state.) I told no one but just continued to pray faithfully about it.

Imagine the excitement I felt a few months later when I saw her walk through the doors of my church. I introduced myself and learned her name was Marlene. The unfolding story of how God would miraculously bring us together through prayer is a great love story—a story of God's love for Marlene and me. God knew just what we each needed in a loving companion for the adventure ahead. Our love story is so miraculous and exciting; surely, it would make a great movie. After all these years, my heart still flutters when I see her enter a room or hear her voice. God did this, and we praise him. Our love story became a part of God's big love story.

Over and over through the years, God has shown himself faithful as he opened his story before us step by step. There have been many answers to prayer, times of deliverance, miraculous healing, and trusting and growing when healing did not immediately come. We have experienced protection, divine guidance, glorious worship, seeing lives transformed, and fantastic fellowship with beautiful brothers and sisters who with us sought the Lord. God gave us the gift of especially wonderful children and grandchildren that Marlene and I love so very much. Each day has had its joys and manifestations of God's grace and care.

Yes, this is a fallen world, so there have been times of great trials, difficulties, disappointments, pain and suffering, and even apparent tragedy. But God has always been there to help us, deliver us, or use all things for his glory and our greater and eternal blessing. When there are hurtful things we don't understand, we remember that we haven't seen the rest of our story yet. When we do, we will see what a significant part of the big story each experience has been.

I know I haven't always lived up to perfect faithfulness, but my God has always been faithful. God knows that my desire is for my life to be all for him. Sometimes when I am in prayer or as I walk through the day, the sense of God's love for me or the conscious awareness of his presence is so great that I feel like my heart would burst or ignite in the flames of his love. What I had searched for I found in God, all and only because of his abundant grace. God longed for me when I resisted, rebelled, and proclaimed my disbelief in him. He reached right over it all and drew me to his love. God sought me until I found him—my Savior, my friend, my lover, and the Lord of my life. I desire to know him in ever-increasing fullness, worship him passionately, obey him faithfully, and let others know of God's great love.

By the way, that group of people whose love and joy touched my heart and opened my eyes? I eventually became their pastor and served them for forty-three years. These dear people were some of the most precious people in the entire world. Who am I to deserve such a blessing? My story is God's love story, and I can live this story for eternity, love without end, joy without end, abundant life forever. This story is my love story.

Chapter 8

What Is at the Center of Reality?

We read in the book of Revelation that the Apostle John had a vision of Christ and heaven. He heard a voice saying, *"Come up here, and I will show you things"* (Rev. 4:1). John saw God on a throne. God on his throne is the center of all things in both the earthly and the heavenly realm. God is the omnipotent Creator, and all things revolve around his purposes. Those things around the throne of God reveal to us something about God and ultimate reality.

We find that John saw several things around the throne of God. What is around God's throne is significant, for this is what is at the center of reality, and what matters. What we see around the throne gives us a key to the heart and purposes of God. John saw twenty-four elders, seven lamps of fire, a sea of glass, four living creatures, myriads of angels, a multitude of saints, worship, incense that was the prayers of the saints, lightning and thunder, a lamb slain, and a rainbow. John saw these things at the center of all that exists. We could reflect much upon each of these, but let's consider just three: lightning and thunder, a lamb slain, and a rainbow, for they are all related significantly.

Around the throne of God, there is lightning and thunder (Rev. 4:5). Throughout Scripture, lightning and thunder have portrayed the presence, power, and glory of God. One such place was Mount Sinai, where God revealed himself in such a great display of lightning and thunder that the people were terrified (Exod. 19:16). How can we begin to comprehend the mighty power of God? Lightning represents well the power of God. One lightning bolt of electricity generates one billion volts of electricity and heat equivalent to temperatures on the sun. God created billions of galaxies, each with billions of suns. What incomprehensible power is this? At the center of reality is the unlimited power of God.

What does this truth mean for you and me? When we face any situation or have any need, God is more than able in his omnipotence to help us and cause us to triumph. Yet, we can worry and fret over the smallest things as if God is too weak to help us. May God forgive us and help us to rely on his limitless power. When we face any circumstance or choice, we can lift our eyes and hearts to heaven and remember that at the center of all things is an omnipotent God.

John saw something else at the throne of God. He saw a lamb slain. *"Then I saw a Lamb, looking as if it had been slain, standing in the center of the throne"* (Rev. 5:6 NIV). *"For the Lamb at the center of the throne will be their shepherd"* (Rev. 7:17 NIV, CEV). Here the heart and the eternal plan of God are revealed. God knew before the foundation of the world that we would sin and separate ourselves from him. God was prepared within himself to be the sacrifice for our sins. At the center of reality is a lamb slain. This truth is at the heart of the great divine romance that is the purpose of creation. This reaching, astonishing love was working in response to Adam and Eve's fall in the Garden of Eden, in God's promise to Abram, in the Temple's design, through the system of ritual sacrifices, and through the law and the prophets. All of these carried a deeper message that God would come himself as a sacrifice for sins. Upon seeing Jesus pass by, John the Baptist said, *" ... Behold! The Lamb of God who takes away the sin of the world!"* (John 1:29).

Yet, there is something even more here. The Lamb on the throne at the center of all that exists speaks of the most significant, profound truth of heaven and earth. What is at the center of reality? Is nothing there but particles of matter and energy waves? Is that all there is? When we are hurt and helpless, are we alone? Is there anybody home in the universe to help us or even care? Is there a place of surety? Is there any place to stand to see things as they truly are? Is there a God? If there is a God, what is he like? Is God impersonal? Is he an evil tyrant?

Here is the most astounding truth that we could ever imagine—no, it's *more* astounding than we could ever conceive—at the center of reality is a lamb slain! At the center of the universe, at the very center of all that exists, is self-giving, sacrificial love! Oh, if our hearts could take it in!

At the center of all of reality is a God who cares, who loves with sacrificial love. God has such self-giving love that he gave his life through Christ as a sacrifice that he might reconcile us to himself. *"In this is love, not that we loved God, but that He loved us and sent His Son to be the propitiation for our sins"* (1 John 4:10). *"But God demonstrates His own love toward us, in that while we were still sinners, Christ died for us"* (Rom. 5:8).

If self-giving, sacrificial love is what is at the heart of reality, this is good news! This news is breathtaking! This truth was a huge part of my inexpressible joy and overwhelming amazement when God, in his grace, delivered me from my atheism and set my heart on fire with his blazing love.

What could bring us more peace? What could give us more hope? What could be more wonderful about what is behind God's creation and what undergirds all that exists? What could be more heart satisfying, more soul-stirring, more life assuring about the essential reality than it is the loving heart of a personal God? Such truth provides a proper context for our perceptions, choices, and aspirations that is inexpressibly wonder-filled and consequential. What could be a more hopeful and fulfilling answer to the question, "What is it all about?" than this: there is at the center of reality, at the heart of all things, a God of self-giving, sacrificial love?

If God were all-powerful but not loving, he would be an evil tyrant. If he were loving, but not all-powerful, he could only give us sentimental support. But God is omnipotent and perfect in love (Ps. 62:11-12), so we have a reason for abundant hope. This fact brings us to our third important truth about what is at the center of reality.

Another remarkable thing that John saw around the throne was a rainbow. *" ... There was a rainbow around the throne"* (Rev. 4:3). A rainbow is a sign of God's covenant, of his promise to his faithfulness to humankind. A covenant is an agreement between two parties. The wonder of this is that God would make such a testament with us as weak and failing as we are. The rainbow is a covenant about God's steadfast purpose and intent for us. God takes the initiative in the covenant and, in his amazing grace, upholds his pledge. God promises to be true in this relationship. If God says it, we can count on it. God displays around his throne the promise of our ultimate hope in his faithfulness.

The Old Testament was a contract based upon law. Since Jesus came, God has established the grace that was behind the law in a new covenant. Christ's shed blood accomplished this for us. The rainbow is about God's heart for humankind and each of us personally. Here is the reason for triumphant hope. God's promises are sure. This sign of God's faithfulness and love is around the throne of God at the center of reality.

The world looks for "silver linings" and sings about things that are somewhere over the rainbow because people look for hope with a longing that was placed there by God. As Christians, we know there is a hope that is real. We know that at the heart of what is real is God's faithfulness and his promise of love to us. There is a rainbow around the throne of God.

God is on the throne, and everything, in the end, is under his control. God's revelation to John was about the glorious truth that God wins. In the end, God wins. If we are his children, we win. In the end, evil is defeated, and righteousness prevails. Love overcomes. God's children win forever. All of history moves to the purposes of an omnipotent and loving God.

"Then I looked, and I heard the voice of many angels around the throne, the living creatures, and the elders; and the number of them was ten thousand times ten thousand, and thousands of thousands, saying with a loud voice: 'Worthy is the lamb who was slain to receive power and riches and wisdom and strength and honor and glory and blessing!' And every creature which is in heaven and on the earth and under the earth and such as are in the sea, and all that are in them, I heard saying: 'Blessing and honor and glory and power be to him who sits on the throne, and to the Lamb, forever and ever!'" (Rev. 5:11-13).

We live in a world where we can experience real trials, bear real burdens, face real difficulties, and suffer real sorrows. But there is a deeper truth than the circumstances themselves. We are not alone, and the larger story is not over. There is a loving God who is with us and for us. At the center of reality is a God of self-giving, sacrificial love who can reach into our circumstances and our lives with omnipotent power and the promise of his eternal faithfulness.

How do we respond to such a God? How do we respond to such love? Love so amazing, so divine, demands our soul, our life, our all.

Chapter 9

The Kingdom of God: A Whole New Level of Living

The love of God is all around us. The love of God holds the very atoms of our world together. By God's love, we take our next breath. Out of God's love comes the most radical proposal ever made to humankind. This proposal is a direct, total answer to our human need. This proposal is the present and the eternal kingdom of God.

Christianity is more than just forgiveness of sins. God's forgiveness for our sins is marvelous beyond our words to express. This forgiveness through the atoning work of Christ gives us access to our heavenly Father and the privilege of being his children. But forgiveness is just the beginning of all that God has for us. Christianity is to be a complete way of living; a whole way of life lived in obedience to Christ.

Christianity is a life lived out of an intimate relationship with the loving and holy God and lived by his grace and his Spirit's power. That's the way it's supposed to be. But I'm afraid Christianity has been watered down so much in our day that some hardly know what the call to Christ means. True Christianity is about the totality of our lives being under the reign of God's love. Christianity is Christ with us, Christ in us, and Christ through us to the world. Christianity is about living our lives in a whole new way on a whole new level, which is a way different from the world's way. Christianity is a way of living with Jesus at the center—not ourselves, not the world, not anything else—Jesus at the center of all things all the time. This true Christianity is the way to find true life, true fulfillment, and a true glorifying of God.

Jesus taught us to pray: "*Your Kingdom come. Your will be done on earth as it is in heaven*" (Matt. 6:10). When we do his will, live it out in love through our lives, his present kingdom comes. Whatever the future kingdom holds for this planet and God's children, there is a spiritual kingdom now into which we can be born. This kingdom of God is the most exciting, most important, most radical proposal that anyone could ever offer us.

People are desperate for answers. Children out of loneliness and despair give into the darkness, take guns to school, and shoot other children. Adults out of desperation and emptiness live lives for possessions, power, or temporary pleasures that do not satisfy. People are looking for something to pull life together and make sense of it all. The answer is living in the way of the kingdom.

Living in the way of God's kingdom affects all that we do. It affects the way we think and the way we talk. It affects our relationship in marriage, our families and the parenting of our children, our work ethic, the entertainment and pleasures we prefer, the use of our time, the stewardship of our resources, and our daily choices.

For many people, God and Christianity are just an add-on—just something on the margin, not at the center of their lives. But Christ at the center of our lives is the only thing that will heal our wounds and bring us to real life. This kingdom living is not something of bondage. Kingdom living is the only way for real freedom; the only way to be all we were meant to be. Kingdom living is not something foreign that is imposed upon us. God created everything to work his way. The world was created by Christ, through Christ, and for Christ (Col. 1:16). It makes sense that life only works God's way. In the end, nothing else really works or truly fulfills.

We introduced the poison of sin by going our way instead of God's way. Now, because we live in a fallen world, we experience troubles, sorrow, and sickness. As we live the way of the kingdom, we bring the hope of a better way to the world. God's kingdom is in operation as we live out God's will and is a partial restoration of what we lost in the Garden of Eden. The kingdom of God is God's heart for the world now that points us to the more excellent experience of a new world coming later for God's children. God created us to live in the kingdom way. To live in line with the kingdom of God is the healthiest way to live. It is the way of the fullest freedom, the most genuine joy, the deepest peace, and the highest fulfillment.

Jesus came to bring into this present world, before what may come later, a spiritual kingdom of God. The kingdom of God was not a marginal issue for Jesus. It was at the center of all that Jesus taught and did. From the first words describing Jesus' earthly ministry (Mark 1:14) to his last words after his resurrection, he was "*speaking of the things pertaining to the kingdom of God*" (Acts 1:3). Jesus declared that he was bringing a whole new way of living, Christ-like living, that would prepare us for an eternity of being his bride.

This emphasis on kingdom living was also a large part of the teachings of the twelve Apostles and Paul. God's Word in Acts 20:25 summarizes Paul's ministry to those at Ephesus: " ... *I have gone preaching the kingdom of God.*" In his last days while in prison, Paul was still "*preaching the kingdom of God*" (Acts 28:31).

Jesus himself personified, embodied the kingdom of God. Jesus came to show us not only what God was like but how we are to live. The kingdom of God is not an impersonal idea or ideal. It is not living by rules and regulations, for this will not satisfy. Kingdom living is living out of a personal relationship with God by the power of his presence. We can live far below our privileges and our possibilities in Christ. God desires to break through into our lives. When the kingdom of God breaks through into our lives, our churches, and our community, many lives will be changed, healed, delivered, set free, and made real. This work of God is his heart and plan. The need in this world is enormous. Somebody needs to seek first the kingdom of God. A group of people somewhere needs to come forward and be all God meant them to be.

How does the kingdom of God fit into the scheme of things in God's creation? We find in God's creation various levels of life, different kingdoms, distinct levels of awareness (or the ability to respond).

The lowest level of awareness or interaction ability would be the *mineral kingdom*. Here we find inanimate, inorganic material. Here there are interactions of fundamental atomic particles, chemical reactions, a response to electromagnetic and gravitational forces, and crystal formation, but there is no conscious awareness. There is no life.

The next higher level would be the *plant kingdom*. Here we have a more substantial response-ability. Plants can respond to light, heat, water, gravity, touch, and even sound with mechanisms we call tropisms. But there is still no conscious awareness, just an automatic response.

A level that has higher awareness than plants is the *animal kingdom*. This increasing awareness is not at all to suggest any kind of evolution. God created things with different levels of perception. Most complex animals have a higher level of response-ability than plants because they have a higher level of neurological development and more mobility.

Higher than the animal kingdom is the *human kingdom*. Humans have the capability for self-awareness, rational thought, elaborate communication, goal setting, philosophy, art, science, technology, and creating civilizations. Humans also have a moral conscience and a spiritual nature because of being made in God's image. This human level of awareness is higher than the animal kingdom (though it seems some may hardly live above the animal level). For many people, the human level is the highest level of awareness and living.

There is an astounding and revolutionary truth that can change everything about life and living. It is this—there is a higher level of awareness, of receptive and response-ability than the human level! This level is the *kingdom of God*. The kingdom of God may be as much higher above the human kingdom as the human kingdom is above the animal kingdom. Living on the level of the kingdom of God is much different than living on the merely human level. Here, we live life on a spiritual level. On the kingdom level of living, there is a whole new plane of awareness and response—a completely new living condition. In the kingdom of God, we do not live by just human reasoning or resources. We live by the very life and spirit of God within us through the continuous presence, power, and guidance of God. We are aware not just through our physical senses, but we are receptive to the supernatural dimension of reality, to the loving voice of God. We are open to the Holy Spirit to enable us to live by God's kingdom principles revealed in his Word.

In this place of abiding in Christ, we live on a new, supernatural, God-prescribed, and God-enabled level of living. This abiding in Christ is the life of living in the atmosphere and experience of God's love and will. No wonder Jesus said, "*seek first the kingdom of God*" (Matt. 6:33). God created us for this. All of our coming to Christ and the kingdom of God is an experience of coming home. When we find this life, we want others to find this treasure too. To revolt against the kingdom of God is to revolt against ourselves. The world has tried. Look at what a mess we are in.

What is serious and sad is that many Christians don't live on this higher level of privilege. Christians miss the abundant life in Christ, and the world does not see an accurate picture of Christ and Christianity.

We can enter and become a part of this kingdom. How? By God's grace through Christ's atoning work on the cross, we enter into this kingdom. God removed the barrier of sin and rebellion that separated us from him. Christ opened the way for us to step into a whole new level of living. God reaches down to lift us to a new life in Christ. When Nicodemus visited Jesus to ask about the kingdom that Jesus was proclaiming, Jesus told him, " ... *Most assuredly, I say to you, unless one is born again, he cannot see the kingdom of God*" (John 3:3). Or, as it may be translated, "unless one is born from above," you cannot see the kingdom of God. We must be born from above into the kingdom of God to this higher level of life. Then we continue to live on this kingdom level as we daily deny ourselves, deny our self being upon the throne of our hearts, deny our self-centeredness, and deny the life of the lower level. We experience this through the cleansing and crucifying work of the cross and the Holy Spirit's power.

It is by the power of Christ's resurrection and the Holy Spirit's enabling presence that we live on the kingdom level. We surrender our lower level lives to live up to the level of the kingdom of God. Christ came to bring us this abundant life. God created us for this full life. We must not be content to live with less. Why should we settle for the lower life when God calls us to live in the heights on a higher plane in newness of life with Christ? Jesus continues to offer this world and each of us "*the glad tidings of the kingdom of God*" (Luke 8:1), and he still bids us seek first the kingdom of God.

So Longs My Soul

Chapter 10

Broken and Poured Out

The design and furnishings of the tabernacle in the wilderness and then the temple in Jerusalem were symbols of God's redeeming work through Christ. There were three courts for the temple—the outer court, the inner court, and the inner-most court called the holy of holies. The inner-most court was where God manifested his glorious presence. Only the high priest would enter the holy of holies through a veil once a year with much shedding of sacrificial blood for atonement for the sins of the people.

God had been waiting for the day when his son, Jesus, would pour out his blood at Calvary, and the veil to the holy of holies would be rent. Then God could embrace us, offering us full access to his presence and love. The veil was torn open by the work of Christ, not only so that we could have access to God, but so God could have access to our inner-most being. According to God's Word, now we who have been born from above are the holy temple of God. "*Do you not know that you are the temple of God and that the Spirit of God dwells in you?*" (1 Cor. 3:16). God has chosen to dwell in a personal way within our hearts, the God-chosen holy of holies.

Here are a mystery and a marvel too staggering to comprehend. The holy, omnipotent, changeless, loving God has chosen to live in the spirits of men and women—our hearts his home! Here is a privilege beyond compare, and a breathtaking reality that must become the most significant, life-shaping feature of our lives!

God made us one whole person, but he intended we live from this place of our heart's communion with him. This fellowship with God would be the place from which the impartations of God's Holy Spirit would be the most significant input by which we evaluate, determine, and integrate the choices of our lives. We can be under the lordship of his Holy Spirit within us, not living by just the input from our physical senses and natural minds.

But something cataclysmic happened to us in the fall in the Garden of Eden. God's spirit separated from our spirits because of our sin and rebellion. This separation from God was spiritual death. Without God enlivening us, our spirits became dormant within us, and we lived by only our heart's choices apart from the indwelling Holy Spirit.

Christ's atoning work removed the barriers that kept God's Holy Spirit from residing within us. God's work by Christ's crucifixion and resurrection allowed us to become alive to God by his spirit. God's Holy Spirit would come and dwell within us. Through the miraculous work of regeneration, we are made alive in Christ as we are reborn. By God's Holy Spirit in us, our spirits are quickened, come alive, and are open to the Holy Spirit's influence. The holy fire of God's presence and love manifest themselves within us. Now we can live by the Holy Spirit within us on the level of the kingdom of God.

We are new. We are different. *"Therefore, if anyone is in Christ, he is a new creation; old things have passed away; behold, all things have become new"* (2 Cor. 5:17). God made us for this living of our lives by his Holy Spirit within. We enter the kingdom of God and become new and spiritually alive by God's grace, by faith that rests in Christ's atoning work. We enter God's kingdom as a child, and we live by child-like faith and wonder, by absolute surrender to the life of Christ within, and by obedience to God's Word and Holy Spirit. If fully surrendered to Christ and the Holy Spirit, ours could be none other than a holy life because our holiness is the holiness of God lived through us.

There is no loss of individuality in our communion with God. God's Holy Spirit does not absorb us into his spirit. God lives in and through our unique and distinctive personalities. In this blessed, intimate communion with God, we become real, truly free, and fulfilled people. We live our lives from the sacred place of God's presence within.

God once manifested his presence in the holy of holies of the tabernacle. Now we are the temple of God, and our bodies and spirits become the holy of holies of God's manifest presence. When Paul wrote, "Do you not know that your body is the temple of the Holy Spirit who is in you?", the word Paul used for the temple is *naos*. This word referred to the inner-most holy of holies of the temple where God manifested his presence and glory.

The mystery, marvel, privilege, and importance of this are beyond our hearts to grasp or words to express! The God who created the stars and planets and all that is, the God we rejected, the Christ we crucified, has chosen to live in us in a life-changing fellowship of love and life! Jesus said, *"he who loves Me will be loved by My Father, and I will love him and manifest Myself to him. ... My Father will love him, and We will come to him and make Our home with him"* (John 14:21, 23).

Christ in us by the Holy Spirit is not just for our joy and fulfillment. It is so that the Holy Spirit of God within us, the love of Christ, might be released through us to others. Through his people's lives, God desires to reveal the wonder of divine love and bring light and life to this injured world.

It is too often true that those who have the Holy Spirit within them by the new birth still live chiefly by the dominion of the outer person of the body or soul. Although the Holy Spirit comes into our lives at conversion, we can continue to live mainly by our flesh. Our bodies and minds are not evil or insignificant. They are a beautiful gift of God. Jesus took on a real human body, and someday we will have bodies that live forever. However, this outer part of who we are is not to have authority over our lives. God desires that we make our choices and live our lives from the God-indwelled place of our spirits, that we be under the loving and life-giving control of the Holy Spirit.

Mary broke an alabaster jar of costly perfumed oil and poured it out on Jesus, and the house filled with the fragrance of the oil (Mark 14:3; John 12:3). Just so, we must be broken in our outer person. We must break the domination of our wrong desires and the input of our physical selves so that we might depend upon God and his Word and his Spirit. Then the fragrant perfume of God's Holy Spirit can be lavished back upon Christ in true worship and released in love upon those around us. This divine love is the only healing balm for a wounded world. This release of the Spirit is the fulfillment of who God meant us to be and how he intended us to live. This work of God fulfills his plan for the world. Here is real life: experienced and shared. How can we express the privilege of being the dwelling place of God, the wonder of life in fellowship with him, or the adventure of being the carrier of God's love to the world? It is beyond words.

No person can be all that God wants them to be or fully accomplish all that God wants them to achieve until they are broken. God can use to the fullest measure only those who are broken and humbled before him and who are trusting him in all things.

Grace, love, and the Holy Spirit of God break the outer person of self-dependence. Sometimes, difficult circumstances crush us so that God may take us away from reliance upon ourselves to reliance upon him. The outer person breaks as we deny ourselves and embrace the cross for the crucifixion of our fallen, rebellious, un-Christlike nature. The outer vessel is broken as we wait upon God in love, as we obey his sacred Word, and as we open ourselves to the presence and guidance of God's Holy Spirit.

In God's presence, we see that apart from him, we can do nothing. The fire of God's love and holiness convince us that only he is worthy to hold the first place in our lives and that only by trusting in his grace and power will we be able to live a fruitful Christian life. The God who calls us is the very one who enables us by his Holy Spirit. God is with us every step of the way to brokenness. As we make him lord of all, God takes us from brokenness to true wholeness and the abundant life that he intended for us. We walk in the confidence that is God-confidence. We live in the fulfillment that only comes by Christ.

God created us to be his dwelling place and to reveal his love and glory through our unique personalities. God is looking for a person or a group of people who are willing to be broken in their self-centeredness and self-dependence, who will surrender totally to him and wholeheartedly trust and obey him. These are those who will gloriously display the life of Christ.

May we be broken and poured out for the love of Jesus. May we pour out of our spirits our treasured store of love upon Christ in sacred worship! May we release the heavenly, fragrant, healing oil of God's love upon this world to fulfill his eternal purpose and glorify his name!

Chapter 11

We Are God's Treasure

" ... *The kingdom of heaven is like treasure hidden in a field, which a man found and hid; and for joy over it he goes and sells all that he has and buys that field*" (Matt. 13:44). This passage of Scripture is one of the most preached upon, taught about, and appreciated scriptures of all of God's Word. A parable is a story told to teach a lesson or truth. Jesus often taught by using parables.

The traditional interpretation and application of this parable go like this: When we find Jesus and his kingdom, we find a great treasure. The treasure is so valuable and wonderful that we should desire to give all we have to possess this great treasure. This interpretation sets forth a significant and life-changing truth. The treasure of Christ is worth everything—worth giving all that we have. This application illustrates my own spiritual experience. I once was an atheist, but when I found Christ, (when I opened my heart to Christ reaching for me), it was the great find of my life. I wanted Christ, and I wanted to be his with all of my heart. There is a treasure: it is Christ and his kingdom, and it is worth everything to possess.

Another interpretation and application of this parable are just as suitable to the words given, and even more valid as it fits into the full story of God's plan. Sometimes parables may have more than one application. Jesus may have intended the traditional meaning. Even so, I believe this parable speaks to us something else.

The one who finds the treasure is Christ. Jesus is the one who finds a treasure. The field in which he looks for and discovers the treasure is the world. Now get this: You and I are the treasure! We are the treasure found in a field! Our great God steps into the field of this world. He puts down the plow of love and grace into the soil of the events that make up the stories of our lives. God turns over the soil of our situations and circumstances. He pulls back the dirt of the deceptions that keep our true selves hidden. He finds us there.

God is the one who finds the treasure hidden in a field. We are the treasure he finds. God finds us where we are in our need—unclaimed and unfulfilled. God values us so much that he gave the best he has. God gave the life of his dear Son that he might win back this world from the enemy and claim us for his treasure.

This story is the bigger story—the greater meaning of the parable. You and I are Christ's treasure. God sees and finds us. God calls us his tremendous treasure and proves it with his love.

The man in the parable sold all that he had. Jesus temporarily gave up his throne in heaven for us. Jesus secured his treasure by the tremendous price of experiencing all the strife and tears that are ours. He lived the life we live in human flesh, and then he suffered a brutal and tortured death on the cross (Phil. 2:7-8). *"Knowing that you were not redeemed with corruptible things, like silver or gold. ... but with the precious blood of Christ"* (1 Pet. 1:18-19).

The outpouring of Christ's blood was how the hidden treasure would be redeemed. By God's immeasurable sacrifice, he purchased the field and us—his treasure. God gave the best that he had that he might have us as his own. We are his treasure.

Something more: the Scripture here in Matthew says, *"and for joy over it he goes and sells all that he has and buys that field"* (Matt. 13:44). It was for joy that Jesus did this incredible act of love and redemption for us. What is this joy? In Hebrews 12:2 we read, *"Looking unto Jesus, the author and finisher of our faith, who for the joy that was set before Him endured the cross"* What was the joy set before him? Was it the communion with the Father? Yes. Was it the pleasure of the Father? Yes, but more. That joy was you. That joy was I. We were the joy set before him that caused Christ to endure the cross. For his pleasure in us, his treasure, for an eternity of loving fellowship with you and me, God gave his best. We are God's treasure, and he finds his pleasure in us.

God has always had this love, this desire, and this plan. He calls his people his treasure in his Word from Genesis to Revelation. Before the world was created, from eternity to eternity, we have been on his mind and in his heart. We will always be his treasure.

When we consider the words of Jesus as given in Matthew 6:21, they take on a whole new meaning, a much larger, more glorious meaning. *"Where your treasure is, there your heart will be also."* This vital truth holds for you and me. But wait, this truth applies to God as well. Where God's treasure is, there his heart will also be. We are his treasure. That means God's heart is with us—wherever we are, whatever we face.

Sometimes we face difficult situations. We can know that God's heart is with us because we are his treasure. If things seem to be falling apart around us—all of our earthly security is failing—we can know God's heart is with us. If our heart is breaking, if we are lonely or empty inside, if we are frightened and confused, if we are experiencing sickness or pain, if we are living through the loss of a loved one, we can know God's heart is with us. We are his treasure, and where his heart is, there will be his loving presence, unfailing promise, and enabling power.

What indescribable love this is that God has for us! How can we begin to comprehend it? God is still reaching for each of us, still seeking for us to respond to his love. Here's the question: Are we living as if we are the greatest treasure of God's heart? If we would, it would transform our lives. To the measure that we live as his treasure, we will impact this hope-hungry world.

God says to every person wounded by sin: "Will you open your heart to my love? Will you walk with me and let me take you on a journey to the person you were meant to be? Will you let me be your defender, your healer, your sure rock upon which you can stand? Will you trust me with your life? Will you let me be your greatest treasure? Will you take the good news, the treasure of my love, to this needy world?"

God sees all of our faults and spiritual deformities. Yet, we are his treasures. God, who loves with a matchless, boundless love, invites everyone to open their hearts to him. If we are God's child by grace, he invites us to rest in his love and experience the blessings of being his treasure forever.

How will we respond to such a God—to such incomparable, unfailing love? Surely a God, who treasures us with such wondrous love, can have our love and our lives completely without reservation.

"The kingdom of heaven is like treasure hidden in a field, which a man found and hid; and for joy over it he goes and sells all that he has and buys that field" (Matt. 13:44).

Chapter 12

Self-Denial:
A Key to the Abundant Life

Jesus calls us to live an abundant life in him. The abundant life is a life lived for the fulfillment of the highest, most meaningful purpose one could ever live: to know God intimately in Christ and to glorify him by doing his will and revealing his love. The abundant life is a life lived in the fullness of God's presence within us. It is a life that overflows with God's love and brings this unfailing, life-changing love to the world. Here in this abundant life, we know profound joy, and we discover, experience, and fulfill our real selves.

Self-denial is an essential key to our abundant life. The two concepts of self-denial and abundant life may seem at first opposed to one another. How can denying ourselves bring us to true self-fulfillment? God created us to love and worship him, to joy and glory in his presence, and to fulfill his purpose for our lives. The first sin of humankind was a rebellion against God's will and ways, and such separation from God's loving authority has brought calamity into this world. We experience real life and fulfillment only as we live the way God created us to live, only as we do God's will each day. This experience may sound limiting and even enslaving to some, but those who are endeavoring to experience God's lordship in their lives testify that it is not so. Self-denial sets us free from limiting factors to be truly creative persons of value.

We enter into this abundant life through God's amazing grace and the work of the cross of Christ. We live out this abundant life daily in its fullness with God on the throne of our hearts. As we deny our self-rule to accept God's lordship of our lives, we experience our true selves and freedom to live life the way God intended. With God on the throne of our lives, we can be free from all of the enslaving influences that keep us back from authentic life and liberty in God's incomparable love.

To deny self means to deny ourselves the lordship of our lives. Self-denial is about taking ourselves off of the throne of our lives and placing Jesus there. In every situation, at every juncture of our lives that calls for choice, we let Christ and his way be the determining influence of our lives. At each moment of our options for response or action, we must deny ourselves the place on the throne of our hearts. We can know Christ in this life-giving way. When there comes the choice to think particular thoughts, make certain responses, or take specific actions in any given situation, we must deny our fallen-nature tendencies in order to respond in a Christlike way or to do God's specific will. We must deny our self-centered and self-determined choices in order to obey the Holy Spirit and do God's will and not our own.

God created us to have him at the center of our lives, not ourselves. Only when God is at the center of our lives, only when every choice and every response is measured and guided by God's self-sacrificing love can we be free to make the life-fulfilling choices for which God created us.

Because of our fallen, corrupt nature, we are prone to choose to act in self-centered, un-Christlike ways. Only as we deny these life-destroying tendencies can we experience the life-giving lordship of a loving Christ. Our flesh, our fallen natures, will fight against our denying ourselves to do God's will and live in God's ways.

How can we do this? How can we deny ourselves? We cannot do this in our natural strength. We can try, but we will only fail. The God who called us is the one who enables us. God is the one who must do this work for us, and then he invites us by his grace to participate in his victory. When Christ died on the cross, he paid not only the price for our sins, but he took our fallen nature to the cross with him. As the Apostle Paul writes, *"our old sinful selves were crucified with Christ so that sin might lose its power in our lives. We are no longer slaves to sin. For when we died with Christ we were set free from the power of sin"* (Rom. 6:6-7 NLT). And this work of grace is made ours by the power of the Holy Spirit. The Spirit of God enables us to participate in co-crucifixion with Christ as we surrender our lives in faith to Christ's victory.

The power of the Holy Spirit accomplishes self-denial in us as we relinquish our authority over our lives and surrender in real love to God.

We must choose to let the Spirit enable us as we believe in the grace, love, promises, and power of God on our behalf.

Jesus gave us these remarkable words that hold the key to abundant life: " ... *If anyone desires to come after Me, let him deny himself, and take up his cross daily, and follow Me"* (Luke 9:23). If we would come after Christ in this way of the kingdom of God, in this way of his abundant life, then we must deny ourselves, take ourselves off of the throne of our hearts. We must take up our cross daily. The cross is the instrument which slays the self-life of its power. Then we can follow Christ in obedience to his will in a walk of love and adventure beyond description.

Jesus then gave the only way we can deny ourselves and find the abundant life through grace: *"For whoever desires to save his life will lose it, but whoever loses his life for My sake will save it"* (Luke 9:24). If we are willing to lose our lives because of our love for Christ and for the sake of his glory, then we will find life and find it abundantly.

It is our love for Christ that determines if we will be willing to lose our lives. Our love for God regulates our willingness to lose our lives and deny ourselves, and yet even this love is a gift of God as we respond to his call and open our hearts to his boundless love. Our faulty, earthly love is not enough. We must have a love that is set ablaze by the Holy Spirit. This response to God's call takes a revelation of the immeasurable greatness of God's love for us, a love that overwhelms us and calls our heart to love him in return. We love God because he first loved us, and in this love, we surrender and trust our lives to him.

We will give ourselves to God and his purposes in proportion to our love for him. Our love for God gives birth to our trust in him. Our willingness to suffer for Christ is in proportion to our love for him. If we would love God more deeply, then self-denial would be less severe and stressful. The pain of crucifixion of our self-life comes from our reluctance to give our lives or possessions over to God in trust. Oh, that we would love God with a full, self-surrendering love!

We must be careful in desiring to deny ourselves. We must not focus on self-denial, or we will become preoccupied with the very self we are trying to deny. We must center the aspiration of our hearts on Christ and his kingdom. Self-denial is not what we seek. We seek God himself and the abundant life he offers. We can so give ourselves in love to a cause or a person that we forget ourselves. There is no higher cause than the kingdom of God and no greater person than Jesus Christ. No other purpose or person is worthy of such love or consecration.

Self-denial in this fallen world of sin-damaged people will always be necessary. But victory in Christ and the abundant life he offers will always be available through his unfailing grace.

How can God ask so much of us? How can Christ ask such a great thing of us to deny ourselves, to lose our lives for his sake? Because he knows that what he offers us far surpasses anything else that could ever be given or experienced. God offers us the life for which he created us. God sets before us abundant life, a life with the unsurpassable value of being a part of his purposes and a life that knows the ultimate joy of communion with God himself. This life experiences genuine, creative individuality, and enjoys the love of God forever and forever.

Self-denial is not a grievous, oppressive, life-limiting act. Denying ourselves the ultimate rulership of our lives is to live on a higher level of divine love and supernatural realities. Self-denial is how we experience a more expansive life for ourselves. We do not lose our personalities and individualities in this surrender to God, but we genuinely experience them in their richness, fullness, and value. The world needs to see such genuine lives lived in overflowing fullness. God is beautifully exalted in our lives and to the world as we live this abundant life in Christ.

Self-denial has fallen out of favor in much of modern Christianity. As a result, we lose much of the love, joy, power, and impact of our Christian lives. Some consider self-denial as limiting, as being anti-freedom and anti-life. We must always emphasize the foundational truths of God's goodness and grace that are central to our knowing and walking with God. Still, Christians and the church must again recognize the necessity of self-denial and the cross in the believer's life.

Self-denial by the Holy Spirit's enabling power is crucial to leaving the past life behind and stepping into all of the new life in Christ. Self-denial is essential to living the abundant life in the Spirit that God called us to live. Self-denial is necessary to do God's will, not our own. God calls us to live for his will to be done on earth as it is in heaven. This call is our privilege and our greatest joy.

God is calling his children to the fullness of the life he offers. If we desire to know Christ intimately and love him deeply, let's deny ourselves, take up our cross, and follow him. Let's lose our lives to find them in Christ. Let's lose sight of ourselves and make Christ alone the lord of our hearts and the vision of our lives. This life is life abundant and eternal. Jesus said, " *... I have come that they may have life, and that they may have it more abundantly"* (John 10:10). Let's say "yes" to this abundant life now and forever.

Chapter 13

God's Love Will Triumph over Life's Trials

God wants us to do better than just "alright" in our walk with him. God loves us too much and has accomplished too much for us just to be doing "alright." We indeed live in a messed up, wounded world, but God wants to be God in our lives. As people, as Christians, we can live in a pressed down, defeated place. We can be bothered by so many things. Jesus' words to Martha could be his words to us: *"you are worried and troubled about many things"* (Luke 10:41). Our troubles and not our possibilities can dominate us. Life can be about our trials and not our triumphs in Christ.

I don't want to belittle the difficulties of our circumstances, but God desires for us to enlarge our vision of him and his boundless love. God desires us to increase our perception of our place in his plans and expand our perspective of his promises and power on our behalf.

The Holy Spirit warns Paul that he faces prison and many hardships, but Paul says, *" ... I don't care what happens to me"* (Acts 20:24a CEV), *"that matters little"* (The Message), *"if only I may finish the race and complete the task the Lord Jesus has given me"* (Acts 20:24 NIV). Regarding what the Holy Spirit has told him about the trials he will face, the Authorized King James Version and the New King James Version of the Bible give Paul's response this way: *"none of these things move me"* (Acts 20:24). The value of the tremendous task to which God had called Paul far outweighed any troubles that he might face. We can be moved by too many things that are nothing compared to the value of God's purposes in our lives.

We can be bothered by many things that we allow to interfere with our walk with God and his working through our lives. "Stuff" is going to happen in our fallen world. We can face hard circumstances or be severely afflicted. People may disappoint us or misunderstand us. Although this may comprise an aspect of reality, there is a greater, higher reality. "Stuff Happens!" "Yes, but God loves me!" God's love will triumph over all of our trials. The truth of God's love for us makes an enormous difference in everything we experience. We can be more than conquerors through our love-filled fellowship with Christ.

In the face of all things difficult, all the "stuff" that happens, we can say, "God loves me!" Even though our difficulties are real, God loves us with unfailing love in the middle of our challenges. Paul experienced a lot of "stuff" that was not so good. His trials were, at times, terrible. He was whipped, beaten with rods, stoned, shipwrecked, adrift at sea, and in danger of robbers. He suffered weariness, hunger and thirst, and cold. His family may have forsaken him, and many of his friends left him. Did Paul feel all of this? Sure he did. Did it turn him back? It did not. Not only did he do better than "alright," Paul used it all. In his infirmities, reproaches, persecution, and distress, Paul sensed that his weakness allowed him to be strong in Christ's power (2 Cor. 12:10).

Is this help from God just for Paul? God wants each of us in our difficult times to find our strength in him. As we keep our gaze upon Jesus and our attention on the call and prize set before us, as we rest ourselves in his love, we can find the supernatural courage and strength to rise above our circumstances. Many of our brothers and sisters who share the gospel face severe persecution or execution in some places in the world. These dangers or hardships are part of the risk they are willing to take to spread the good news of Jesus Christ. "So what" has been the answer of many when asked about the dangers and difficulties they face.

There are many excuses that we can give for backing away from God's call. Things can trouble us and keep us from victorious faith.

We may think, "No one really loves me." But God loves us! Nothing else matters more than the truth that God loves us. God created us for himself and his purposes, and he believes in us for who we are in Christ. God's Word says that nothing can separate us from the love of God.

Sometimes we can be easily bothered by what others say about us or the way they treat us. We can be upset about something that is nothing in the light of God's eternal work. Of course, no one likes being rejected or persecuted. Yet, that doesn't need to stop us from loving and following the One who has not rejected us and loves us unconditionally. Remember, people misunderstood and rejected Christ. He knows how we feel. God experiences with us our hurts of rejection. We should stop focusing on what people say about us and focus on what God says about us, what he believes about us, and what he has done for us. *"He who did not spare His own Son, but delivered Him up for us all, how shall He not with Him also freely give us all things"* (Rom. 8:32).

We can say that some people don't believe in the dreams or direction that God has given us. They say that we can't fulfill God's plan, though several mature, trusted Christians had confirmed our call. If God has revealed his desire for us and believes in us, that's what matters. Remember Joseph. He was put in a pit, sold into slavery by those he loved, lied about, had his name defamed, was wrongly accused, put in prison, and overlooked. But God saw him, loved him, and carried out his plan for him. So what if someone else doesn't know our hearts. God sees us, knows us, and loves us! God can carry out his dream and plans for our lives. We are safe in his hands, and only there can we fulfill God's purposes for us. When it seems everything or everyone is against us, we can say, "God loves me!"

Sometimes Christians can't get anything done for being upset with one another. What a shame! People are going into eternity without God, and we can be disturbed over something small in light of God's eternal plan. Someone won't do things the way we like it done, so we just take our ball and go home, or we just find another church where people care about the same trifles we do. The problem occurs when it becomes about us when it's supposed to be about God and his heart, his kingdom, and his glory. We can be a part of the most significant cause: the kingdom of God and God's glory revealed! How about getting lost in that and forgetting ourselves? The set of our hearts can be—"Whatever happens, I'm giving myself to God." "It's about God, not about me." "It's about what brings him glory!"

We can think, "but I am so weak, so limited." God is still the omnipotent God. God is still in charge. The last time I looked, God was still God, and able to do all things in his will for his children. The things we face may seem so big, and we seem so small. But our God is bigger than any problem we face. And, " ... *If God is for us, who can be against us?"* (Rom. 8:31).

The devil fighting? Yeah, tell me something new. But God has defeated the enemy. All he can do is intimidate us.

People may try to thwart us as we try to fulfill God's will. Caleb was delayed a few years (forty years), but God gave him his mountain in the Promise Land.

It may look like things are not going our way, but if we genuinely love God, *"all things work together for good"* (Rom. 8:28). It may seem as if our family is falling apart. It may appear the world is falling apart. But God is still the omnipotent ruler of the universe, and he is our God. God's love for us can matter more than the trials, troubles, and sorrows we experience.

We can say that living a Christian life in this fallen world can be hard. And we would be right. Things really can be tough at times. But what's that got to do with it? What matters is God loves us, and we can be a part of his purposes. What matters about what we are doing is this: "Is it God's will?" "Is it what we are called to do?" "Does it please God?" "Does it bring God glory?" "Does God's love call us to it?" "Does it take us deeper into the embrace of God's unchanging love?" "Does it fulfill God's love for the world?" What does being hard have to do with it?

Eugene Peterson gives the Apostle Paul's words this way: "*Since God has so generously let us in on what he is doing, we're not about to throw up our hands and walk off the job just because we run into occasional hard times*" (2 Cor. 4:1 The Message).

We do not deny the troubles. Life can be trying in this fallen world. There can be huge disappointments. We can experience lingering afflictions and pain, heart-breaking betrayals, consequences of other's disobedience, trials, and temptations. These are real. But God sees us and God cares. God will take us through with strength beyond our own, with a vision of a higher and eternal reality, and with lessons learned about his faithful love.

We must not disregard or belittle the real hurts and disappointments that we or others experience in this fallen world. God doesn't deny or disparage our pain or our hardships. He feels them with us. God meets us at the place of our deepest hurts, our most unrelenting stresses, and our hardest trials to heal and help us with passionate and tender devotion. His love, strength, and divine perspective are bigger and more real than our hardships or hurts. Even though "stuff" happens in our lives, God is there with us in the middle of the stuff to love us, see us through it, and use the "stuff" to make us stronger in Christ.

If we genuinely love people in this broken world, we will know real hurt. Love hurts when the ones we love hurt. God's deep love for us is what took him to the cross. The woundedness that kept us back from life in him was the reason for his act of unfailing, sacrificial love. God's broken heart for our wounded hearts was experienced and displayed as he hung on Golgotha's tree.

Some hurts that we experience in this life can be gut-wrenching. Some of the hurts are hard to understand from our limited, earthly perspective. You know your difficulties and disappointments. God sees and cares about all the hard things you face.

You may have experienced betrayal by a trusted friend or others to whom you were devoted. The wound is deep. Jesus knows about betrayal by friends and is right there with you.

You may have been misunderstood and lied about when you knew your motives were right and pure. So was Jesus. He knows how you feel.

You may have suffered the terrible trauma of verbal, physical, or sexual abuse. God knows your heart and knows the wounds go deep, but his healing love can go deeper still and bring you to wholeness.

You may be experiencing extreme stress in a bad situation from which there seems no way out. When it seems there is no way, God can make a way, or he can see you through it with a peace that *"surpasses all understanding"* (Phil. 4:7) and use the situation to make you more like Christ.

You may be experiencing a financial need or even disaster. You feel crushed for not being able to provide for those you love. Know that God sees you and loves you. Just keep trusting him. Be honest and willing to take whatever steps are right in God's eyes and keep yourself in his hands.

Whatever happens, he will be there for you. He never comes late in his plan.

Your marriage may be disintegrating despite all of your prayers and trust and efforts. You know God's desire for marriage, and you feel guilty about your situation even though others have made choices that were out of your hands. God sees you there. He will not forsake you as you seek his face and give yourself to him.

You may be suffering in affliction and pain. You and others have prayed and believed God for healing, but healing has not yet come. Know for sure God is with you. He cares about your pain and will heal you now or later. Until he does, he will meet you with the comfort and peace of his presence and the promise that your afflictions are but for a moment and are achieving for you *"an eternal glory that far outweighs them all"* (2 Cor. 4:17 NIV).

Maybe you are going through the disgrace of a significant failure. God still loves you with an unchanging, unfailing, unconditional love. In his love and forgiveness, you can have a fresh start in an intimate walk with him.

You may have experienced the death of a loved one. Such loss is one of the deepest hurts anyone can suffer, especially if it is the loss of a lifelong marriage partner or a child or grandchild. Only God knows the depth of your pain. He feels it with you. When the words of others can't bring the comfort you need, the presence of God and the embrace of his love will help you take the next step and lead you into hope for the future and the eternal life he promises.

Even when it seems God is nowhere near in your most profound sorrow, God is there. He will not forsake you. The darkness and clouds will clear, and you will see the light of his presence again. If you have decided to follow Jesus, by his grace and help, keep going toward the light that you know is beyond the darkness. The love of your heavenly Father will lead you to where all is well.

In all of your hurts and hardships, Jesus knows how you feel and cares more than your heart can understand. If you are his child, he is with you in every situation to hold you in the arms of his love, heal your wounds, and lift you to his presence to see eternal realities.

At Calvary, on that old, rugged, terrible cross, God the Creator opened his heart in Christ to take upon himself all of our sins and sorrows, all of our hurts and failures. There, at the cross, we see God's open wound of love. At Calvary, Jesus, in his limitless love and infinite mercy, enfolded our wounds into his wounds and shared our every hurt as his own. On the cross in real pain in a manner beyond human comprehension, God revealed to us a self-sacrificing love that will not let us go. The prophet Isaiah wrote of this work of Christ. *"Surely He has borne our griefs and carried our sorrows"* (Isa. 53:4). Then in his resurrection, Christ showed us that he had conquered all sorrows, all sickness, all suffering, all evil, all our earthly hurts, and even death itself to bring us real life in him now and in heaven forever.

This is a God who understands our hurts, who feels our sorrows. This God will see us through to victorious, abundant life, and the eternal joy ahead for all of his children.

Stuff happens in this world—sometimes, hard stuff. Sure it does. But above it all, in it all, through it all, God loves us. This truth is why our intimate relationship with God has such an impact on our lives. Here, at this place of sacred communion with Christ, his strength becomes our strength, his faith becomes our faith, his promises become our promises, and his love becomes the preeminent reality of our lives.

I have experienced some difficult times. My only sister, a single-parent mother of two children, was brutally murdered by an intruder in her home. My family has sometimes misunderstood me. Friends have betrayed me. God has miraculously healed me of several physical needs, but other times I have suffered severely painful afflictions for what seemed a long time. Through it all, God has been with me to see me through, strengthen me, and teach me valuable lessons of trust, faith, and love. We must not let troubles keep us from a glorious fellowship with our God or from fulfilling his purposes.

Too many Christians can give up their commitment to God when they meet disappointments, troubles, prolonged afflictions, or conflicts. We must not give up our hope. *"We often suffer, but we are never crushed. Even when we don't know what to do, we never give up. In times of trouble, God is with us, and when we are knocked down, we get up again"*

(2 Cor. 4:8-9 CEV). We must not turn aside from the purposes of God or the blessing he is setting before us. Jesus is always there to help us on to his will as we love him above all things and trust in his unfailing care. We can never live this Christian life on our own anyway, even when it's not hard.

Being a Christian is a supernaturally lived life from the beginning. We make it to God's fullest work and blessing as we moment by moment open ourselves in love and trust to his grace-given, supernatural operation in our lives. We cannot take one step in this way of the Christian life without Christ's life within us by the Holy Spirit's presence and power. This privilege is what God has won for us and what he offers us along our journey with him. In his arms of love, we are safe for eternity.

How much do we love God? How much will we trust him, and how important are his will and his glory to us? Oh, that we would love God enough, trust him enough, to allow him to take us on to all he has for us despite the troubles or difficulties we may face! Oh, that God's love would so overwhelm us that we would press on with his help through every difficulty! Oh, that we might be able to declare with Paul, "*since we have this ministry, as we have received mercy, we do not lose heart*" (2 Cor. 4:1). May we be able to say with Paul that "*none of these things move me*" (Acts 20:24) "*if only I may finish the race and complete the task the Lord Jesus has given me—the task of testifying to the gospel of God's grace*" (Acts 20:24 NIV). We must run the race, whatever happens. Too often, our lives are about our comfort and convenience, and we are turned aside by things that shouldn't matter in the light of God's eternal purposes.

How can we be faithful and victorious, no matter what happens? There are biblical stances that you and I can make real in our lives to go forward to God's work and blessing. Our spiritual victory is not determined by our outer circumstances but by the inner stances of our hearts.

We can have a *purpose* that is worth the price—a mission so magnificent it is worth any God-approved cost. We have that purpose in Christ and the kingdom of God. We can be utterly committed to Christ and the expression of his life to the world. There is no higher purpose.

We can have a *passion* that moves our soul. We can have an overwhelming longing above all other desires to love God with all our heart, soul, mind, and strength and be filled with his love. We can get close to God's heart, to the fire of his passion, which compels us to take his love to the world.

We can have a *perspective* that allows us to grasp something of who God is and what he offers us. We can see from God's point of view. From this place of vision, we can see that God is greater than any difficulty we face, and he can work even our trials into the beautiful fabric of his will and blessing for our lives.

We can have a *power* that is greater than our own. We need a power that is greater than our natural strength. God "*is able to do exceedingly abundantly above all that we ask or think, according to the power that works in us*" (Eph. 3:20). Paul faced many hardships. How did he handle them? "*I can do all things through Christ who strengthens me*" (Phil. 4:13).

We can have *promises* from our God that we can stand upon in confidence. God has promised to love us, take us through all the hurts and difficulties of life in this world, and use all things to bring us deeper into his love and further into his purposes. God has given us precious promises in his Word that sustain us through every circumstance, every trial, and every wound we may experience. The Bible is full of assurances of his love and care, whatever we face. (See Deut. 33:27; Ps. 55:22; Isa. 41:10, 13; 43:1-2; John 16:33; 2 Cor. 4:17 and 1 Pet. 5:7.)

Paul gives us a tremendous promise in his letter to the Romans of the sufficiency of God's love. "*Who could ever separate us from the endless love of God's Anointed One? Absolutely no one! For nothing in the universe has the power to diminish his love toward us. Troubles, pressures, and problems are unable to come between us and heaven's love. What about persecutions, deprivations, dangers, and death threats? No, for they are all impotent to hinder omnipotent love. Yet even in the midst of all these things, we triumph over them all, for God has made us to be more that conquerors, and his demonstrated love is our glorious victory over everything! So, now I live with the confidence that there is nothing in the universe with the power to separate us from God's love. I'm convinced that his love will triumph over death, life's troubles, fallen angels, or dark rulers in the heavens. There is nothing in our present or future circumstances that can weaken his love. There is no power above us or beneath us—no power that could ever be found in the universe that can distance us from God's passionate love, which is lavished upon us through our Lord Jesus, the Anointed One!"* (Rom. 8:35, 37-39 TPT). Embraced in the changeless, limitless love of God, we can be more than conquerors.

Most importantly, we can know that we have a *person* with us: not just any person, but God himself, who spoke the universe into existence and calls the stars by name. We have a God who loves us with infinite, unfailing love and watches over us with infinite, unfailing power. We can know this God in intimate fellowship, and in this sacred communion, we find our hearts at rest and satisfied. In our human limitations, we may not have the answer to all of life's mysteries, but we can have God. He is the Answer. Job sought answers for all of his suffering. God didn't answer his questions, but when Job saw God himself, he was satisfied. This answer was all he needed, for God was what would fulfill his longing heart. God is what we need to see us through any situation and bring us to the fullness of life.

Christ himself is all of this for us. Christ is our *purpose, passion, perspective, power,* and the surety for all of God's *promises. " ... He has always been and always will be for us a resounding 'Yes!' For all of God's promises find their 'yes' of fulfillment in him"* (2 Cor. 1:19-20 TPT). A person can grow to know Christ so intimately and love him so deeply that there is overall contentment in life regardless of circumstances (Phil. 4:11-13).

There comes a time when we should make a choice to take a step of faith into a higher plane of living. By the grace of God, as we surrender to him, we can live by the purpose, the passion, the perspective, the power, and the promises of Christ. For God's glory, we can say with Paul, "none of these things move me" when faced with difficulties and trials. We can say, "God loves me!"

Someday we will walk in complete victory. We will be with the One for whom we fought the good fight and ran the race. There will be no more earthly hardships or sorrow or pain for God's children because "*God will wipe away every tear from their eyes; there shall be no more death, nor sorrow, nor crying. There shall be no more pain for the former things have passed away"* (Rev. 21:4).

God doesn't make light of our hardships and trials in this world; they matter to God, and He cares more than we can know. He's the one who sees us through our trials and transforms them for our good. We can use the "stuff" in our lives as Paul did. We can grow in our trust in God and, in our weaknesses, become stronger in Christ's power. Overwhelming victory can be ours by the surety and power of God's love. In his boundless love, God brings us through to the glory of his presence and his eternal purposes.

One day we will see face to face the One for whom we ran the race. We will look into the eyes of the One who has loved us with infinite, unfailing love, and we will know that it was worth the race. We will be glad that we declared in the face of our trials, "Yes, but God loves me," and that we said with Paul, "none of these things move me."

So Longs My Soul

Chapter 14

Holiness Is Not an Option

"You shall be holy, for I the Lord your God am holy." Leviticus 19:2

Holy living is not just something we can choose as an option, thinking it is not essential to our Christian walk. If we are to live a full Christian life that pleases God and fulfills God's purpose for us and the world, then we must walk in holiness. Holiness is not optional. It is not an add-on or an extra. It is the heart of who God is and the hallmark of God's true people. It is essential to who we are as children of God and vital to our walk with God.

Because of Christ's work at Calvary, we know that God sees us as righteous in Christ; but, by the same grace that saved us, God calls us to live out this way of holiness personally and daily in each for our lives. I am sorry Christians have messed it up so badly. Christians and the church have given holiness a bad name. Now is the time in this hope-seeking world to live as God has called to live. It's time to experience holiness as God meant it to be lived, to reveal it in a way that lifts the loving Christ to the world and shows the real heart of God.

An article in my daily newspaper a few years ago caught my attention. It was alarming. The caption was: "Sin Is Now Macho in Great Britain." I can tell you—sin is not a sign of true manliness in Great Britain, America, or anywhere else. Sin is death, no matter how you dress it up. God calls us to fulfillment in a life of Christlike purity.

Holiness may be out of fashion, even in the church, but that doesn't change God's nature or God's call to our hearts. If holiness is out of fashion, I'm afraid the church has more to do with it than anything or anyone else. The church has often given a false picture of holiness. Our long faces, rules to follow, legalism, coldness, and judgmental and condemning attitudes are contrary to the loving, joyful, adventurous life in Christ. We have even at times in the church equated holiness with the way we wear our hair, makeup, and jewelry. Holiness may affect how we dress, for we want to reflect Christ to others, but it is not so much about how we wear our hair as it is how we wear our hearts.

The devil's deceit and, I'm sorry to say, the hypocrisy and lack of love in the church can trick us into almost believing that holiness is something we don't want anyway. The enemy is happy about this because it means the church will miss the abundant life that God offers, and then so will the world.

What has happened? First, the church turned the world off to holiness by her hypocrisy, lack of love, and lack of a genuine relationship with the living Christ. Then, when the world ridiculed and rejected holiness, well, the church herself rejected holiness. Now the church runs from holiness about as fast as the world. How sad and serious this is! When the church is more proud of her "broad-minded" worldliness than her privilege of purity, you know something is wrong. And if we don't avoid holiness as Christians, as the church, then we do something else. We believe it is an extra, an option, an add-on like heated seats or racing stripes for a car or seven additional speeds on a food blender.

Holiness is not an add-on, not just an option. Holiness is at the very heart of true faith and true Christianity. If we genuinely love God, then we love what God loves, and God loves holiness in his people. We are to be holy because our God is holy. The Apostle Peter wrote, *"as He who called you is holy, you also be holy in all your conduct, because it is written, 'Be holy, for I am holy'"* (1 Pet. 1:15-16).

What does it mean when we say God is holy? God is separate from his creation. Though not separated from his creation by love or interaction possibilities, God created all things distinct from himself. God is not a part of the universe. Nature may reveal something of his holiness, but God transcends it. Holiness is who God is in himself apart from creation. Holiness speaks of God's high moral excellence and perfection. God doesn't conform to a standard of morality; he is the standard.

Holiness relates to and embraces every other attribute of the Godhead. All that God is will be manifested in his holiness, even his boundless love. His manifested holiness is his manifested glory. His holiness makes him mysterious, numinous, and even terrifying—terrifying as his holiness inspires overwhelming awe and wonder. Isaiah saw God upon his throne and heard the seraphim cry, "*Holy, holy, holy is the Lord of hosts; the whole earth is full of His glory!*" (Isa. 6:3). Isaiah's encounter with God was so overwhelming that his response to the presence of such perfection and holiness was to cry, "*Woe is me, for I am undone!*" (Isa. 6:5).

What does it mean for us to be holy? It means we are set apart to God and all that he is for us and through us. We entirely consecrate ourselves to God, who is holy. In Scripture, the words holy, consecrated, and sanctified (and even saints) all have a root word of *being set apart.*

For us to be holy means that we are set apart to God so that we have the likeness of God in his holiness, in his moral excellence, and abounding love. His excellence and love are discovered in his Word, revealed by the life of Christ, and brought to us and through us by the indwelling Holy Spirit. Our holiness is the revealing of God's nature in our lives. The Word of God becomes flesh in our lives and is demonstrated through us for God's glory.

Holiness is not just about us avoiding sin or following rules. It is about following and revealing a person—Jesus Christ. We are set apart to Christ, and he makes his life known through us to the world. Most simply—holiness is Christlikeness. It is a life lived as Christ lived in love and obedience to the Father. Jesus came to show us what God the Father is like in his holiness, but he also came to show us what we can be like as we live in a love relationship with him. God waits for someone or a group of people who will hunger for all he is and all that he offers.

Salvation is by grace alone through faith, but God desires that we grow in Christlikeness and bear the fruit of the Spirit through our lives. God longs that we "*grow in the grace and knowledge of our Lord and Savior Jesus Christ,*" as Peter exhorts us (2 Pet.3:18). We don't earn our salvation through our lives of holiness. We can never live in God-equaled perfection in this fallen world in our fallen natures. But Christ has set the ideal pattern for how we are to live. We do not fulfill our lives and God's purposes unless we endeavor to live like Christ. Such a way of living can only be ours by God's grace and by the power of the Holy Spirit within us. Only Christ within us, living through us, can meet God's standard of righteousness.

There is no righteousness in us. Our holiness is God's holiness shining out, lived out through us as we are set apart to him. Our holiness is Christ within us and lived through us because we give ourselves to him in surrender and because the Holy Spirit saturates us. The Holy Spirit is, indeed, the spirit of holiness. Holiness is not even good acts of our self at the center of our lives. It is Christ at the center. It is Christ with us, Christ in us, and Christ through us to the world.

How can this life of holiness, of Christlikeness, be lived out personally, intentionally, and practically in our lives? Can such a thing be done? Can such a holy life be lived? Not by ourselves. Not one of us can live this life on our own. God must do it. As we truly set ourselves apart to God, he lives his life and love through us. By the miracle of God's grace, we can live this life he has called us to live.

At this place of possibility and privilege, we face the greatest danger and sin of the Christian life. In desiring to live a pure and holy life for God, we can become self-righteous, and the greatest of blessings becomes the greatest of sins—that of pride (which can be followed by a judgmental attitude toward others.)

Our privilege of a holy God dwelling in us and living through us is because of the grace and work of God through Christ. Our place is only stepping aside, surrendering to Jesus so he can live through us in our unique personality because of his barrier-removing work on the cross. We have nothing of holiness in and by ourselves. Our Christian walk is all because of the righteousness of Christ and his indwelling by the Holy Spirit. We can only walk in the privilege of Christlikeness as we humble ourselves in brokenness and desperation before God and acknowledge that he alone is the source of our life.

To know God intimately is to know him in his holiness. To love God is to love God in his holiness. Anyone who truly loves God with all of their heart will want to live a life of Christlikeness—not for show, not for the praise of others, not for a sense of accomplishment, not for pride's sake, not to try to earn anything from God but in response to his love. Because of our love for God, we will long to align our hearts with his heart and bring joy to his heart. What God cherishes, we cherish. God cherishes holiness. God's life of holiness lived through us is what delights him, honors him, and reveals him to the world.

Every Christian should desire to live a holy life—a life of Christ living abundantly through us—not to make the experience about us but that it would be all about God. We desire this for the sake of his glory and his work in the world.

We shouldn't be anxious or stressed about our desire to live a life set apart to God—trying to measure ourselves and our Christian walk by self-constructed lists or attempting to determine what we can do and still be holy. God wants us to serve him in childlike trust, wonder, and delight. But we should be desperate for God and his loving, life-changing work in our lives. When our hearts are captivated and captured by God's love, we desire to please him—not out of bondage, but out of love. We want to live according to his Word and his heart. "What pleases Jesus?" is the question we ask. "What honors God?" "What increases my love and devotion to him?" "What reveals who he truly is to those around me?" "What shows the hope of what he offers to a lost world?" "What displays his holiness, his loving heart to the world?" This display of love is where we find life's joy and fulfillment and where God is truly honored and glorified.

To live a holy life is not life-crushing bondage. It is the freedom to be who we were meant to be. It is our freedom to live the way God intended us to live. It is life with the fullest adventure. To live a holy life is not a denial of life—it opens the door to abundant life.

" ... *Be renewed in the spirit of your mind, and that you put on the new man which was created according to God, in true righteousness and holiness"* (Eph. 4:23-24). The Message paraphrases it like this: "*take on an entirely new way of life—a God-fashioned life, a life renewed from the inside and working itself into your conduct as God accurately reproduces his character in you"* (Eph. 4:23-24 The Message). According to God's Word, this is holiness, the holiness we want, and for which God created us. Until we desire it—until we have it—the world will not want what we have. The life we offer will be no different from the world's way of living.

Research through surveys about the similarities and differences in behavior between Christians and non-Christians in categories such as sexual purity, divorce, gambling, home life, and entertainment has often shown no significant difference between Christians and the world. These things should not be. It is no wonder the world doesn't want what we have. We don't have anything. If Jesus is at the center of our lives, if we are living by his Word and by his love, if it is "no longer I but Christ," there should be a difference in our lives. We don't want walls that separate us from touching the world with God's love, but we should have a distinctive and inviting life that shows the world God's heart.

Until we see ourselves and the world as God sees, we are not likely to be disturbed by conditions around us (as long as they don't threaten our comfort). The problem is we have learned to live with unholiness—not just in the world but in the church and our own lives. We have come to consider unholiness as almost acceptable and expected. We aren't much disappointed or even concerned when we don't find holy living in the church, our own lives, or others' lives. Then we wonder why there is no power in the church and why there is no fruit in our lives!

Holiness, holy living, has become no longer a part of our idea of Christian life or our heart aspirations after God. Our approach to explaining our faith to the world can be this: "I am just like you. I live just like you. I have just asked God to forgive me; that's the only difference." No. A thousand times, no! Yes, God forgives us. Praise God for his amazing grace! But we are also a new creation. Old things have passed away; all things have become new. There has been a regeneration inside of us that is to work out into our character and conduct. Real Christian living is holy living. It is the holiness and love of God lived out through us to reach the world as we surrender ourselves to the indwelling Christ.

God is holy. God has made holiness and holy living the necessary moral condition for the health of his creation. God has designed things this way. Someone has said, "Whatever is holy is healthy!" Evil is a terrible moral sickness that ends in death. To turn from God is to turn to chaos and ruin, eventually for eternity.

Our word "holy" comes from an old Anglo-Saxon word that means "well, wholeness." God's concern for the universe, and particularly and personally for you and me, includes the moral health that is real life. Because God's love for us is so boundless, he cares if we experience the authentic life for which he created us. That is why he is vehemently against all that is not holy.

The judgment of God, the wrath of God, against sin is real, but it is also right. God's wrath is set against sin because unholiness takes away the health and wholeness of those he loves. Oh, how the enemy warps the truth! We can believe a lie while all the world waits to find hope for real life.

Because God is holy, he hates sin. We often say, "God hates sin but loves the sinner." Too often, we rush over the first part to get to the second. God hates sin because he loves us, and he values us. If God didn't treasure us, it wouldn't matter to him whether we sinned or not. We may excuse our sins, but God detests them. Every time we sin by living contrary to his Word, his will, and his love, we are doing something God abhors. God judges sin because it keeps us from real joy, fulfillment, and fellowship with him.

God's hatred for sin is like a mother would hate a disease that would take her child's life. This life-taking disease is why God hates sin. Christ loves us with an immeasurable love that wants the best for us. God's astounding love is why he desires holy living for his children. We can say it doesn't matter, but it matters so much to God that he sent his Son to die a cruel death on the cross so we might be delivered from sin and live holy lives.

We need to cultivate the same hatred for sin that God has while nurturing the love he has for everyone. There is much around us to deaden our sensitivity to what is pleasing to God. Some tell us that we shouldn't have guilt because there is no such thing as sin. But the answer is not to declare we don't have guilt because we believe there is no sin. The answer is that we are guilty before God, but there is forgiveness—being set free with a clean slate to start fresh with our choices and experience life as God intended.

Holiness is not an option—not an extra. Holiness is at the very center of the abundant life and is required for a continuing and growing intimate fellowship with God. Holiness is necessary for personal fulfillment. It is the only way to be a whole person. Holiness in our lives is required for God to accomplish his will and glorify his name fully. Fruitful service demands holiness. Holiness does not earn our salvation. We can't begin to be holy until we have become Christians because it is Christ's life within us that is lived out through us.

Our salvation is by God's grace through faith in the work of Christ. But if we are not living holy lives and have no desire to live holy lives, we may not have partaken of his grace. The same God, the same Holy Spirit that draws us to salvation, draws us to Christlikeness. It is the same drawing of God. A person can't say, "I am drawn to have my sins forgiven, but I am not to drawn to Christlikeness." If you have no drawing, no desire, no hunger for holiness, no longing to be like Jesus, then you and the world have a right to question your salvation.

It is vital to understand that God has called every Christian to a holy life. There are no exceptions to this call. Holy living is not just for pastors, missionaries, and Bible teachers. Every Christian, in every nation, whether he or she is rich or poor, learned or unlearned, young or old, a plumber, a banker, a student, a doctor, a nurse, or a busy housewife, all are called to live holy. And, what's more, everyone is summoned to be as holy as anyone else. We have different callings and responsibilities, different levels of spiritual maturity, but God calls all of us to be equally holy to fulfill our place in the body of Christ. There are no exceptions. This privilege of great joy and abundant life is for all.

God has opened the way for us to experience the life and power of holiness and be all he has created us to be. God gives us the most astonishing, most glorious invitation that anyone could ever receive. In love, he reveals to our hearts the problem of our lives. Then, he sets before us the answer that discloses the breathtaking secret at the heart of reality. God invites us to hide our unholiness in the wounds of Christ. On the cross, Christ's heart was torn open to reveal the unfathomable love of God. Just like God hid Moses in the cleft of the rock when he revealed his glory to him, in Christ, we take refuge from God's judgment against sin in God himself. At the center of the universe is self-giving, sacrificial love. We come to God and plead the merit of the blood that Christ shed for our unholiness. As we are hidden in Christ, God sees only the righteousness of his Son. All of this work of God is by his divine love, grace, and favor. Then in this same grace, as we present ourselves to God in a continual surrender, God begins to work in our lives so we can partake of and then reveal his holiness. It is God in our unique personalities as we consecrate ourselves to him.

Holiness is not just a matter of giving up things. It is the thrill of discovery—of finding God, our true selves, and life in the kingdom of God. Holiness is not restrictive—it is renewing. It is not grievous—it is glorious! It is not losing—it is finding true life and fulfillment. It is Christ in us and through us to the world. Jesus lived, died, rose again, and ascended to the Father to intercede for us and send the promised Holy Spirit that we might know this authentic and eternal life in God.

For those who are not true Christians, this is the invitation to the life for which God created every person. Nothing else will ever satisfy.

For those who are Christian, holiness is not an option, not an extra. What God calls us to, he will enable us to do. There is no such thing as true Christianity without holiness—only a cheap attempt to escape from responsibility. God waits for our love. He longs to reveal himself to the world in the awesomeness and majesty of his holiness.

Christianity is a continual growing in Christlikeness by God's grace, presence, and power. As we live in holiness, our hearts are open channels through which God can touch the world with his love. May our souls hunger for holiness and the living God for the glory of his name!

So Longs My Soul

Chapter 15

Whatever Became of Carnality?

"For you are still carnal. For where there are envy, strife, and divisions among you, are you not carnal and behaving like mere men?" 1 Corinthians 3:3

Paul is writing to the church at Corinth. The church has a high calling and a great opportunity. The people of the church are very gifted, but they are also very carnal and in danger of missing their calling.

Corinth was one of the most important commercial cities of its day. The large city was at a crossroads for shipping and commerce that traveled east and west through the Roman Empire. But Corinth was also a place of great immorality. At Corinth was the temple to Aphrodite, the goddess of sensual, lascivious love. The name "Corinthian" became a by-word for that which is debased and immoral.

Paul lovingly pleas for the church to be holy and set apart to God. He desires for God's people, God's church, to be a light in a dark world. We do not live in Corinth, but we do live in an ungodly age. We, too, have the opportunity to be light in the world. We could miss our calling for the same reason as the church at Corinth—not because the world is dark or evil, but because of the evil in our own hearts.

Several years ago, Dr. Karl Menninger, a well-known psychiatrist and founder of the Menninger Foundation and the Menninger Clinic, wrote a book entitled, *Whatever Became of Sin?* The premise of the book was that we couldn't separate our mental health from our moral health. He desired to bring the psychiatric profession back to the idea of personal accountability. He proposed a revival of personal responsibility in all our human activities. His book caused quite a stir.

There are many ways that we can excuse our bad behavior, so we have no responsibility. We can explain our conduct by our genetic make-up, by our hormones, by environmental or situational pressures, by health issues, or by our family background. Some of these factors may provide the context for our choices, but alone they leave no place for personal responsibility for our actions or our character.

A few years ago, in a California city, a man borrowed money from a bank. He invested and unwisely spent the money. What did he do? He sued the bank because he said it was their fault because they should have known better than loan him the money. People do not want to take responsibility for their choices.

We can make choices. We are responsible for our actions. Menninger's book asked the question: "Whatever became of sin?" I would like to ask another important question: "Whatever became of carnality?" It has gotten to the place where we hardly ever hear about it. Just as the world doesn't speak of sin—as if it doesn't exist—Christians and the church don't speak of carnality—as if it doesn't exist. Whatever became of carnality?

Carnality in Christians arises from our fallen natures. Because of our sin-corrupted natures, we have an inner bent to sin and an aversion to God and his ways. We acquired this fallen nature because of Adam's rebellion and disobedience and our own choices. The term carnal is used in the general sense to mean that which relates to the crude, bodily pleasures and appetites. According to the biblical concept, we are carnal when we rely upon or govern our lives by the fleshly desires or corrupt attributes of our fallen nature.

God is trying to get us to a blessing—to everything he has for us, to all he meant for us to be. He wants to live through us, through his church, to be a blessing to others. God wants his matchless, measureless love to flow in abundance through his people to the world. He can't do that as he desires because of carnality in the hearts and lives of believers. It's time to face the real problem so that we can experience the real cure. We need to know about our sickness so we can acknowledge the remedy.

To be carnal—to live by our flesh—is to be dominated by our sinful nature, or our own fleshly, un-Christlike desires. We could even live by our "good" selves on the throne of our lives and not by the spirit of God within us. Carnality arises from that within us that is opposed to God. Paul describes the conflict between the flesh and the spirit in his letters and gives the life that is lived by the Holy Spirit's conquering power as the answer. He writes to the church at Galatia and all of us: " ... *Walk in the Spirit, and you shall not fulfill the lust of the flesh, for the flesh lusts against the Spirit, and the Spirit against the flesh; and these are contrary to one another"* (Gal. 5:16-17).

Carnality comes from that inner disposition that draws us to pull away from God and his will. Paul wrote, "*the carnal mind is enmity against God"* (Rom. 8:7). Carnality is that which, if it has control, will impel us to be mean, hateful, self-centered, self-exalting, self-pitying, overly sensitive, judgmental, unloving, unkind, unforgiving, unlike Christ, and open to the temptations of the world. Carnality incites us to rebel against God's authority and all authority. Paul further describes the fruit of our desire: " ... *for where there are envy, strife, and divisions among you, are you are not carnal?"* (1 Cor. 3:3).

This nature which opposes Christlikeness we acquired because of the fall of humanity in the Garden of Eden. When Adam and Eve separated themselves from God by rebellion and disobedience, we became warped inside. We became poisoned. This poison draws us to live with self on the throne of our hearts rather than God, to act in ways opposed to God and ways that are unlike Christ. We are each responsible for our carnal behavior, for we don't have to be slaves to our fleshly or sinful nature. There is a way out that God has provided to live in the Spirit and not by the flesh.

It is vital to know that to live by the carnal nature is not the way that God meant for us to live. God did not intend for carnality to define who we are. Who we are in Christ is the person God desires us to be. God made us for his kingdom—to live his way—to be like Christ in our unique personalities. This life is the fullness of life.

However, because of rebellion and disobedience, we have this poison within us. It is awful. It is deadly. It robs us of joy, hope, the full experience of God's kingdom, and being the real people God intended. Carnality in our lives robs those around us as well.

The world is not the church's biggest problem. It's not what we face in this world that is our greatest hindrance, even though the evil around us grows ever worse. Carnality is the church's most immense problem. It's this poison within us. This carnality in the church is why she is lifeless and powerless. The greatest hindrance to the effective sharing of the good news with others may not be the devil or the world but carnality in the lives of believers. God can't fully trust himself or his kingdom to people who are ruled by the carnal nature.

Carnality is the chief cause of problems in the home, marriages, the family, the church, social institutions, and eventually the world. We must resolve this issue of the rebellious, unconquered self-will that refuses to surrender to God's loving and life-fulfilling will.

If we are going to become the Christians God calls for us to be and if we are going to be the church God intends for us to be and if we are going to be the witness the world needs for us to be, we must be healed and delivered from this terrible disease of carnality. Jeremiah declares, "*they have healed the hurt of the daughter of My people slightly*" (Jer. 8:11). We need a more than slight healing of this sinful nature that is opposed to God.

The good news is: there is a cure! There is a way out! God gives us the remedy in what he has done for us in Christ.

We can ask the question: "If carnality is a significant problem, and is our most grave illness, why do we hear so little about it?" Whatever became of carnality? How little we hear about it in best-selling Christian books or even from most pulpits. Yet, our fallen nature is our problem.

Why do we not hear more about it, when God's Word seems clear on the subject? Maybe some think it is proclaiming salvation by works, but it's about how we live once we become Christians. Perhaps some Christian leaders don't understand the centrality and seriousness of this issue for a Christian or a church. Could some preachers or teachers live with carnal traits in their own lives and don't want God's light to shine upon them? Maybe spiritual leaders don't love people enough to confront the problem, or perhaps they don't have the courage because some have been attacked severely by carnal people when they try to point out the need. If you pick on carnality, you can stir it up. Or, maybe we don't consider the issue of carnality because we choose to turn to naturalistic explanations for our behavior. Our circumstances can give the setting but are not God's spiritual explanation for our un-Christlike behavior.

Problems caused by this carnal nature are tragic. This God-resistant nature is why we live defeated lives, our witness has little impact, and our churches are often powerless. Because of this issue, there is no powerful move of God in individual lives and no worldwide harvest of born again people for Christ.

Whatever became of carnality? I'll tell you: we have made up excuses for our meanness so that we don't have to take responsibility for it. We have proposed all kinds of reasons for our bad behavior. Whatever became of carnality? We can be mean and despicable and blame all sorts of things. We are tired or under stress, or we are just a "sensitive" person. We are misunderstood or mistreated, or we have a bad family background. But the reason we act in self-centered ways is because of this bent to selfish behavior in our hearts. We can say "I'm just being myself"—as if when "being ourselves" is unkind, that's okay. But it's not okay. "That is just the way I am," we can say. For heaven's sake, let's not brag about it if it's not like Jesus. We can say, "I am just being honest" when we are judgmental. Well, if it's hurtful and not redemptive, let's just be quiet. We can act in anger or an abusive manner. We can run over others to accomplish our goals, and we can explain it as just being passionate about our cause. Since when is rightful passion an excuse for un-Christlike behavior that is not pleasing to God? Might it be that we are not rightly passionate at all, but we just want our way? We can get upset at people and call it righteous indignation. Often there is nothing righteous about it. Someone just punched our "button," and we are offended. We can want to straighten people out, not out of love for them, or to be redemptive, but just to justify our anger or make us feel better ourselves.

Someone may say, "I'm sorry I acted that way. I had a bad day." But when will someone just be honest and say, "I'm sorry. I was being carnal?" We need to know the problem to receive the cure. God will help us, but we must not hold on to our poison.

We can blame others or blame our circumstances, and not face the real problem. Circumstances do not cause us to be carnal. They just reveal our carnality and bring out what is in the heart. We are all weak, and we often can fail, but that is why we cast ourselves onto God's abundant grace. We recognize the problem so that God can help us and deliver us to a more Christlike life.

We must understand that people have sometimes been genuinely hurt and abused, and it takes time for healing. God knows, and he is loving and patient in our healing, just as we should be with others. We must not carry the guilt for all of our wounds, but we can all look to God for our healing and deliverance.

We all can sometimes, or often, fall short of Christlikeness. Wallowing in guilt, getting discouraged, and giving up is not the answer God has for us. We can take heart because God has a way out of our bondage to our carnal nature. It's about getting to the freedom of being the real people God means for us to be. It's about being the channels of love God intended.

According to God's Word, there are three types of people: the natural person, the carnal person, and the spiritual person. The natural person is the person who lives on the natural level whose spirit is dormant before a new birth regeneration. God may bring a person into his family, but they can still be carnal, still be self-exalting, irritable, unkind, unforgiving, fault-finding, or contentious. We can say it doesn't matter, that we are just human, that we have been forgiven of past sins and are now Christ's. But it does matter! It matters for the blessing of our fellowship with God, for God's ability to use us to accomplish his will, for our witness to a life-seeking world, and ultimately it matters for the honor of God's name. How many will miss their eternal destiny with God because we refused to live and witness from the place of Christlike love?

God desires to work in mighty, world-changing ways through each of our lives and his church, but the carnal spirit hinders his working. It doesn't have to be. God calls us to be spiritual people—to live supernaturally, minute-by-minute on the level of the kingdom of God.

The spiritual person is not perfect or self-righteous. Self-righteousness is the worst of all sins. The spiritual person is weak in himself but strong in God, leaning entirely on him. The spiritual person surrenders to God and his lordship. In humility, he or she endeavors to live by the Spirit and not by the flesh. The cross crucifies the former person so God can resurrect the new person in Christ. Buried in the likeness of Christ's death,

God raises us to a new life in the likeness of Christ's resurrection (Rom. 6:5).

Whatever happened to carnality? It is still there—ruining our lives, destroying our relationships, devastating our marriages, disappointing and wounding our children. Carnality hurts those we love, demolishes our witness to the world, hinders our churches, and holds God's mighty work.

Is there a remedy? In Romans 7, Paul describes our struggle. In Romans 8, he gives us the answer. We live by the power of the Holy Spirit and not by our flesh. There is a cure for our malady. By the cross of Christ and the work of the Holy Spirit, Christ provided a way for us. Christ's death on the cross was not just atonement for the forgiveness of our sins, but was for us, as we are in Christ, death of the old person enslaved to the Adamic nature. Then, through his resurrection and the work of the Holy Spirit, we experience the creation of a new person in Christ Jesus.

We participate in this death and resurrection to experience a new life lived by the Spirit (Rom. 6:3-6). We must deny the carnal nature by the power of God's Holy Spirit and take those terrible traits of our spiritual fallenness to the cross. "*Those who belong to Christ Jesus have nailed the passions and desires of their sinful nature to his cross and crucified them there*" (Gal. 5:24 NLT). God enables us to do this by his Spirit as we surrender ourselves and these carnal traits to him. The God who invites us to this spiritual life is the One who enables us. (Rom. 8:2). If we wrestle in our own strength for this victory, this resurrected life, we only become frustrated and give up in defeat or think it is impossible, so we live as "*mere man*" as Paul describes it (1 Cor. 3:3). The flesh will never crucify the flesh. Carnality will never crucify carnality. Only as we surrender ourselves and this carnal nature to the work of our crucifixion with Christ will we begin to experience what Paul declared to the Galatians: "*I am crucified with Christ: nevertheless I live*" (Gal. 2:20 AV).

How can this be lived out personally, practically, and intentionally in our lives? This life is not beyond our reach but is the invitation and promise of God.

There are crisis experiences for many believers along this way of living the Christian life. These are times when we get a fresh revelation of God's love and our carnality and unholiness. We see our desperate need of God, and our utter inability to live in Christlikeness by our strength. We come to God and claim a fresh and more in-depth work of his grace. However, this Christian life should be for all of us a continual growing process. It will be a daily and an ever-increasing surrender of ourselves and our un-Christlike nature to God for an ever-increasing experience and expression of Christlike living and an ever-growing appropriation of Holy Spirit enablement.

The love of God for us is vast beyond all measure. God knows that we are only fulfilled in a relationship with him and in doing his will. That's the way God created us. God longs for us to know all of the blessings he has for us and to experience his presence and love in increasing fullness. He knows that this bent to sinning in our hearts can keep us back from this full fellowship. God's love for us took him from heaven's glory to the torture of a cruel cross, not only so we could have our guilt removed, but so that our hearts might be turned from our carnal ways to his freeing, fulfilling love. God, in his boundless love for us, desires this intimate fellowship with us. " ... *He died for all, that those who live should live no longer for themselves, but for Him who died for them and rose again"* (2 Cor. 5:15). What a wonder is this fantastic privilege!

All that God is and all that he has done for us should compel us to love him with a love that wants all barriers to our fellowship with him removed. We want all hindrances taken away to his working through our lives to touch the world with his love. God's Holy Spirit calls us and then enables us to embrace the cross for a carnality-defeating work of love. We can choose this way into real life. We can say "yes" to God's full delivering work in our lives if our greatest desire is to know God intimately in Christ and glorify him by doing his will and revealing his love. Such a work of grace is available to each of us.

Knowing God's great love for us, the terribleness of the carnal nature that is enmity against God, and the consequences of living by our fallen nature, we cannot, we must not be content to allow this fallen nature to control our lives. We know our possibilities of a more victorious spiritual life, and that God has made us a way of deliverance. If we had cancer and someone offered a sure cure, would we refuse it? If we had taken a deadly poison and someone offered us an antidote, would we not take it?

Our cure for carnality begins with recognizing the need. We acknowledge that there is something better for us, and we hunger for it. There is a work of God that can bring us to our true selves, to deeper fellowship with God, and a more extensive offering of our lives for God's glory. We make no excuses. We come to God with our need, our thirst for him. We acknowledge our poison. We humble ourselves before God in brokenness and faith. We give the unsurrendered parts of our lives to God and the work of the cross and his Holy Spirit. We believe the promises of his Word for his work of deliverance for our lives. We live daily in consecration and the appropriation of God's divine help. We discover God meets us at the place of our surrender and offers us victory and the life he meant us to live. God, himself, is our deliverer and fulfillment.

What a possibility! What a promise! What a privilege! What a life of victory lived in the love of God! What a wondrous God of amazing grace and unfailing, measureless love! Oh, that we would see the tragedy-causing terribleness of our carnal nature! Oh, that we would love God enough that we would want absolutely nothing to interfere with our relationship with him or our witness to the world!

Whatever happened to carnality? May we fully recognize the debilitating and life-destroying effects of our carnality on our fellowship with God and our living the Christian life in true Christlikeness! Only as we live in this liberty of Christlikeness will we be a compelling invitation to the world of the freedom and fulfillment found in Christ's love. Let the church acknowledge carnality as a chief obstacle to fulfilling the mission of lifting Christ to the world. Let us in desperate hunger, real humility, and expectant faith surrender ourselves to the sanctifying work of the cross and the Holy Spirit so that God can be honored and his love revealed through our lives. God's fiery, faithful, boundless love for us and our ardent love for God could be satisfied with nothing less than our total surrender to God's purifying grace. Such an experience of shared passion and abundant life would bring a revolutionary, glorious move of God to the church and the world.

Chapter 16

Flies in the Ointment

We are called to impact our family and friends, neighbors and co-workers, our nation, and our world with God's presence and power. We want to touch those around us with God's love and grace. This work is God's, but we are his instruments. To significantly and eternally impact this world, we must be a sweet aroma of Christ to those around us. *"Our lives are a Christ-like fragrance rising up to God. ... To those who are being saved we are a life-giving perfume"* (2 Cor. 2:15-16 NLT). Sometimes instead of a sweet aroma, we can release a terrible odor, a rotten smell.

My wife and I decided a few years ago that we wanted to feed the squirrels around our woods-encircled home. We got a squirrel feeder and placed it in our back yard. We filled a barrel with corn to use for the squirrels' food and covered the barrel with a lid to keep out the rain and birds.

One day that summer, I noticed an awful odor behind our house. I wondered what it could be. The next day the aroma was more potent. In a few days, when I walked out back, the smell was even more terrible. There was something rotten on Seven Oaks Drive where we lived, so I searched for the source of the rancid, obnoxious smell. The stinking aroma seemed to be coming from the barrel of corn. When I took off the lid, the odor nearly knocked me off of my feet. I found a monstrous, churning cauldron of maggots that were moving in waves of rottenness! The smell was overwhelmingly sickening. I put on a mask, drug the barrel deeper into the woods, and poured it out, gagging and heaving. It was bad. (I hoped no one would call a chemical spill alert or call out the National Guard.) I flushed myself off with a water hose, washed my clothes, and wondered if I would ever get rid of the smell.

What we had hoped would be a gift for us and our neighbors—playful squirrels close by—had become something else altogether. Because I had left the lid partially off of the barrel—uncovered and unguarded for a few days—rainwater had gotten in and soaked the corn and something so small as a few flies had caused the whole barrel of wet corn to spoil, fill with maggots, and become an awful offense.

"Dead flies cause the ointment of the apothecary to send forth a stinking savour" (Eccles. 10:1 AV). We believe Solomon is the author of these lines. In Ecclesiastes 9:13-20, Solomon considers the way of wisdom. In Ecclesiastes 10:1, he describes how a little foolishness can spoil one's reputation and honor concerning wisdom. This verse, this picture, can also be used to illustrate another valuable spiritual principle.

In Solomon's time and even to this day, the apothecary was a person who prepares medicinal and fragrant compounds. The apothecary was also the name of a place like a pharmacy or a drug store where a person could get healing medicines, aromatic ointments, perfumes, scented soaps, sweet-smelling balms for refreshment and healing, or perfumes and incense for worship.

Imagine a father whose beloved daughter—the treasure of his heart—is very ill and suffering in great pain. He takes off for the village to seek some soothing, healing ointment. The small town is full of sights and sounds and smells with which he is familiar. He sees vendors at their places selling fruits, vegetables, pottery, or wool-woven clothing. But these are not on his mind. These are not what he is looking for this day. He needs a remedy for the hurt of someone he loves. He hears the sound of the vendors as they cry out, the braying of the donkeys, the bleating of the sheep and goats, and the voices of the people who know him calling out his name. This day he moves on. He smells the fragrance of cooking and spices, and the not so pleasant scent of the camels. The sun is hot. The air is dry on his throat. The dust rises in little puffs around his sandaled feet as he hurries quickly through the streets. He is looking for a place he hopes will have help for the one he loves.

He finally arrives at the apothecary. In his small village, it is just a tent flap open to the street. He rushes quickly to the proprietor and asks for a perfumed, healing ointment for his sick daughter. This apothecary is the place that he hopes will have, is supposed to have, the help and healing ointment for which he is desperately looking. "My daughter is ill," he urgently pleas. "I need some perfumed, healing ointment." "I'm sorry, my friend," the vendor responds. "The pot was left unguarded. The top was off, and a fly got into the ointment. It has begun to spoil and rot. There is no healing, no help here for you today."

One fly can infect an entire jar of aromatic, healing ointment. What was supposed to be fragrant and bring healing was putrid and repulsive. What disappointment! "Dead flies cause the ointment of the apothecary to bring forth a stinking aroma."

We, as Christians, are to be a sweet perfume to God and the world. But if we aren't careful and leave our hearts unguarded, bad attitudes enter—love-blocking sins, help-stopping self-centeredness, cure-curbing arrogance—poisonous, hurtful things. It was like when I left the barrel of corn unguarded and uncovered for a few days. Flies got in and caused rottenness that made it stink. Toxic, harmful things get in the heart and cause the smell of something rotten in our lives. People in this world are looking for hope and healing. Too often, they are disappointed. Too often, they don't find the healing they are searching for in the church or the lives of Christians.

Paul said we are to be a sweet savor to God and a "life giving perfume" to the world. But if we let sinful things, things unlike Jesus into our hearts and let them linger there, there rises to our God a stench that grieves him more than we can know—even though, and especially because He loves us with a measureless love.

This malodor breaks God's heart for his children and others, others who need his healing through us in a broken, wounded world. Our lives can smell of death and rottenness to those God wants to reach in love through us. God knows that others see him as we portray him.

We are to be a sweet smell to the honest and hungry-of-heart of this world. Life, for most people, has lost its taste. People are hurting and empty. People are looking for healing, hope, real meaning, and genuine joy in their lives. People are looking for the sweet perfume of a loving Jesus. We are to bring the smell of healing, hope, meaning, and joy to the world. Instead, too often, our hearts are left unguarded, and our lives become contaminated and send forth a repulsive aroma. The church has become repulsive to many in this world. For some, this is because they reject Christ's claims and the message of the cross. Even the sweet savor of the loving Christ is distasteful to them. But for many, the church is repulsive because she often has "flies" in the ointment that "send forth a stinking aroma."

Do you know what makes dead animals, and old wet corn, stink? Bacteria. The rotten aroma is the smell that bacteria release as they consume an organism. Sin, self-centeredness, and living in a way unlike Christ can devour our hearts and lives, and as they do, they release a stench to heaven and the world.

Living contrary to God's way soils us. Humanity is looking for a way to be made fresh and clean. People are seeking a beautiful aroma to fill their hearts and lives to refresh their weariness. Men and women are searching for a balm of healing and comfort for their wounds. We Christians have the balm of Gilead! We have a loving, life-healing Christ within us to share with the world. But "dead flies cause the ointment of the apothecary to send forth a stinking aroma."

We must be on our guard against flies that would spoil our healing balm. We must keep our hearts fresh and clean in love and purity and guard against flies that would ruin our ointment. We can't let the flies stay in our hearts. There is too much at stake. We need to identify the pollutants and deal with them by the work of the cross and the power of God's Holy Spirit. A general consideration of the need will not do. We must deal with each rot-causing thing specifically and intentionally. Only as we name the flies in the light of God's love will we experience freedom and perfume-procuring wholeness in Christ.

What are some of the flies that can spoil our ointment? Let's name a few. A bountiful presentation of God's Word would support the stench-causing danger of each one: murmuring and complaining; harsh, unkind words; critical, judgmental spirit; gossiping; cantankerousness; contentious spirit; irritability; uncontrolled temper; envy (greenfly); resentment and bitterness; unforgiveness; self-pity; stinginess; fear; secret sins; impure thoughts; impatience; and pride. These un-Christlike attitudes or behaviors can "cause the ointment of the apothecary to send forth a stinking aroma."

How do we deal with these things that pollute our experience with God and our witness to others? We look to, and we make ours, the work of God's grace in our lives by the sin-destroying work of the cross and the cleansing and enabling power of the Holy Spirit.

Our love for God determines what matters to us about the way we live. Because of God's unchanging, boundless love for us and because of our own genuine, whole-hearted love for God, our greatest desire should be to live in intimacy with him, to glorify him in all things, and to let him live through our lives in a way that proclaims the wonder of who he is to this world.

We must identify the things that are infecting our lives. We must then acknowledge them as critical things blocking our full fellowship with God and our correct portrayal of our loving Savior to the world. Our love for God cannot bear for these infectious things to be in our hearts. We come to God and specifically acknowledge and confess these hindrances—broken-hearted over our ways that betray his love, dishonor his name, and hinder his cause. We bow before him helpless in our ability to deliver ourselves, but expectant in our faith for his loving, emancipating work. We subject these un-Christlike traits to the crucifying work of the cross and the Holy Spirit's cleansing work. We allow God's all-powerful presence to push out daily the corruptive behaviors as we look to God in love. It is in surrender to the life of Christ within that we overcome those things that keep us back from a full experience of all that Christ has won for us. Then daily, hour by hour, we submit ourselves to a loving God, and we live abiding in his love by the Holy Spirit within us.

This glorious possibility is why we worship with abandonment, pray with passion, bathe ourselves in the Word of God, plead the blood of Jesus over our lives, and live together with others as the Body of Christ. We seek to be filled continually with the Spirit. This privilege of purity is why we must be careful to guard our hearts and keep the cover of Christ's blood over us. God's Holy Word says: *"Keep your heart with all diligence, for out of it spring the issues of life"* (Prov. 4:23).

It does little good to look for a spiritual harvest if we are not willing to be the sweet savor of the love of Jesus. We may wonder why God doesn't work more openly, why we don't see more people step into a new life in Christ, why we don't see those we love and people in our community touched by God in a greater way, and why we don't bear more fruit personally in our lives. It may be because of God's always best timing. What we don't want it to be is because there are flies in our ointment.

Are there flies in our ointment? Have our hearts been left unguarded? When people encounter our lives, what do they smell? Is it the sweet aroma of Christ's love? We may have been a Christian for years, but are our lives an accumulation of flies or grace? Have the years made us send forth the sweetness of Jesus or a stinking aroma? What if churches were full of people whose lives consistently released the sweet perfume of Christ's love? This love would bring a spiritual awakening to the world.

It's time to remove the dead flies, empty the barrel of maggots, and reveal the love of Christ to the world. God calls us to fill every place we go with the sweet aroma of the love of Jesus Christ and the good news of the kingdom of God. The world is needing the precious perfume, the restorative balm, the healing ointment that is Christ. God is looking for a person or a group of people through whom to pour his life into this world.

I am sorry for those who have not become Christians because they have smelled some rotten ointment. If they could only know that this is not the way it's supposed to be. If they would give themselves to live this life as it should be lived, how blessed they would be, and how it would please our heavenly Father. For those of us who are Christians, it's time to be what God has called us to be so that we could reveal the real Jesus to this world.

Once when Jesus was at the home of Lazarus—the man he had raised from the dead—Mary took a jar of expensive perfume made from the essence of nard, and she anointed Jesus' feet with it. Mary had the finest of perfumes. There were no flies in it. She had kept it guarded in a precious alabaster box. When she broke open the jar to pour the perfume on Jesus' feet, the Word of God says the house was filled with a beautiful fragrance. May we be broken and poured out with the pure, fragrant, healing presence of Jesus. May we be a Christlike fragrance rising to God and a life-giving perfume to those who seek real life!

Chapter 17

Keep Your Heart with All Diligence

My walk with God has been an amazing and blessed journey. God has helped me many times in many ways. There have been challenging places, terribly hard times, disappointments, betrayals, and unwished-for afflictions (like everyone may experience in a fallen world of human free will). God has been with me through it all to help me walk in greater trust and richer experience of his love. As I look back, I see how, repeatedly, God had mercy on me, intervened for me, and was all the while getting me to his purposes. Sometimes he worked in answer to specific, trusting prayers, sometimes through the lives and obedience of others, and sometimes by the grace of his loving providence.

I know my life has been in his hands. The delight of fellowship with him and the wonder of his working in my life have been an inexpressible joy. If anyone finds anything more exciting, fulfilling, joyful, or important than an intimate walk with the almighty, holy, Creator God, please let me know. I am entirely confident that nothing will ever be found more wondrous than knowing and loving God. There is nothing more important than glorifying God by doing his will and revealing his love in the power of his Spirit.

After all these years, I believe I stand on the edge of even greater wonders of God's love and work. I sense all the more the importance of my heart being given entirely to God and being kept his by a continual surrender to his unfailing love. God's Word sets before me an essential key to all of the adventure that lies ahead. *"Keep your heart with all diligence, for out of it spring the issues of life"* (Prov. 4:23).

In a walk with God, it is possible, even right, that we are both desperate and joyful at the same time. We are desperate for God himself above all else. Our heart is desperate for God's help, for God's work in our lives and the world for his glory. At the same time, we are joyful in Christ and excited, for we know that God's promises are sure, his power is limitless, and his love is unfailing. We can trust ourselves to his care and his plans for our lives.

After all of God's help and blessings, after years of Christian service, after many battles and victories, I am still in danger of not guarding my heart. After all these years, my cry is that my heart remains guarded and kept for God and his will. I desire that my heart be pure and holy in Christ that I might be a carrier of God's love and grace to this world. Only a heart kept for God can be much used of God. My heart-cry at this place in my spiritual journey is this: "God, deliver me from a hard heart, a cluttered heart, a cold heart, a trustless heart and a small heart." They are simple things, but they are vital to experiencing all that God has for each of us and his work.

"God deliver me from a hard heart." "God save me from a heart that has become hardened to your speaking voice and your loving call." God wishes to speak into our lives by his Word and his Spirit. What an incomparable, inexpressible privilege! God desires to call us daily into the continuing adventure of his will. However, struggles and weariness, the hurts we experience along the journey, disobedience, or the sin in our lives can cause our hearts to be less sensitive to God's voice, less trusting of his promises. Our successes can cause us to depend upon our thinking, our abilities, and our resources so that we neglect or even reject God's guidance.

May we allow God to help us to always have a tender, sensitive, responsive heart to his leading! In our alertness to God's loving presence and guidance, we find the way to God's true blessing and God's work through our lives. Genuine servants of God like Abraham, Moses, Elijah, David, John the Baptist, Mary, John the Apostle, and Paul were all very different in their personalities. Yet, they all had one thing in common: they had a heart that was responsive to God's love and God's voice. When God called, they responded, and God used them mightily for his glory. The words of the writer of Hebrews quoting from Psalm 95:7-8 are God's words to me and each of us today: "*Today, if you will hear His voice: do not harden your hearts.*" God deliver us from a hard heart.

"God deliver me from a cluttered heart." So many things contend for our attention and affection. A cluttered heart is a divided heart—a heart divided by its allegiance to many competing calls. God calls us to a heart single in its devotion to him and his purposes. We are to genuinely and continually seek first the kingdom of God. We complicate our lives when we don't order them around simple truths and don't eliminate those things not oriented to these truths. We simplify our lives as we seek God first as the center and wellspring of our lives. *"Blessed are the pure in heart, for they shall see God"* (Matt. 5:8). The word "pure" here means that which is simple and unmixed or unmingled with other things like pure gold is made up of only gold.

The Apostle Paul said, *"This one thing I do"* (Phil. 3:13 AV). We often would have to honestly say, "These many things I do instead of seeking first the kingdom of God." God deliver me; deliver us all from a cluttered, divided heart. May we get free of all that distracts us from eternally significant living and focus on what brings us to a simpler life of loving, trusting, and obeying God.

"God deliver me from a cold heart." Christians, even those in leadership, can become cold in their relationship with God. Numbed by disappointments or betrayals, we can lose the flame of love that should burn fiercely for our God. We can become distant from God in our affections and apathetic to the needs and lostness of others. We should, and we can have a heart on fire for God and ablaze with his love and presence. God calls us to have a burning passion for what is on his heart: the eternal welfare of the lost, the care and victory of his people, and the advancement of his kingdom.

We can become distant from God even though he tenderly calls us to draw nearer to his flaming love. Jesus' words to those in Ephesus were, *"you have left your first love"* (Rev. 2:4). This forsaking of our love for Jesus doesn't have to be true of us. We can have a passionate hunger for God himself. Our hearts can burn with longing for what is on God's heart—the triumph of his church, the revival and the edification of his people, and the salvation of the lost of this world who are without hope and without Christ.

We can allow many things to put out the fire in our hearts: the spirit of the world, Satan, other people, the church, or ourselves by negligence or disobedience. We must be intentional about seeking God and his heart.

We must hunger for the fire of his manifested presence and his measureless love. Paul wrote to the church at Rome: "*let us keep the fires of the spirit burning, as we do our work for the Lord*" (Rom. 12:11, J.B. Phillips). "*Be enthusiastic to serve the Lord, keeping your passion toward him boiling hot! Radiate with the glow of the Holy Spirit and let him fill you with excitement as you serve him*" (Rom. 12:11 TPT).

We don't earn this spiritual fire. Christ won this privilege for us by his work on Calvary. We can place ourselves next to God's flame. We can open ourselves to his Holy Spirit fire by our genuine hunger, real surrender, and expectant faith. Our desire should be to plunge into the depths of Christ's love—into the all-consuming, all-fulfilling fire of his burning love. God deliver us from a cold heart.

"God deliver me from a trustless, wonderless, unchildlike heart." We can lose the wonder of who God is and what he has done for us. We can lose the awe of the manifold beauty of his creation, the measureless depth of his love, and the marvelous miracles of his work. We can outgrow the wonder of the ever-new adventure of walking with God. We can become skeptical of his faithfulness. We can lose our childlike heart of trust— trust as a tender-hearted child might have in his or her loving father. To lose the wonder is to lose the joy, the hope, the excitement, and the open doors to God's gracious gifts and miraculous working.

"God deliver me from a small heart." May God deliver us from a heart too small to take in all he could do and desires to do in our lives, in his church, and this world! Our God is big, and he can do big things for his glory. Not that we should be seeking "big things" for their own sake or to satisfy our egos, but may our hearts be big enough to believe God for all of the great things on his heart. From a big heart, our faith in a big God allows us to pray big prayers for marvelous, mighty things which he will do. God has a miraculous work of his grace and power for each of us, for those we love, his church, and spiritual awakening in this world. What could God do for his glory if our hearts were big enough to receive it? God who created the galaxies, the God who called Abraham and made of him a nation, the God who parted the Red Sea for his people, the God who sent his own Son into the world to bring us eternal life, this God can do all that is on his heart. " ... *With God all things are possible*" (Matt.

19:26). May we have a heart big enough to grasp what God is big enough to do!

God is looking for a person or a group of people with hearts kept for him. He will come into their hearts and through their lives with his manifest presence and power to accomplish his purposes. If we passionately desire to know God intimately and love him deeply, we want to keep our hearts with all diligence. May our fervent heart-cry be "Lord, give me a tender heart; a single heart—uncluttered and undivided; a warm heart—a heart on fire for you and with you; a childlike heart; and a big heart. Grant me a heart that is an open and prepared channel for releasing your boundless love to the world."

How can this be? How can our hearts be kept for God? The God who calls us enables us by his Word and his Spirit. We meet with God in his Word. We pray. We live in Worship. We abide in the place of his presence. We are clear with God and all people. We are around people with kept hearts. We guard carefully the doors to our hearts—our ears, our eyes, and our minds. We continually surrender to God and his purposes. We claim a fresh, manifested filling of God's Holy Spirit each day. We set our hearts toward God. He will meet us in the sacred temple of our hearts by his grace and for his glory. May God forever be praised!

So Longs My Soul

Chapter 18

Overcoming the Enemy

In considering the great love story between God and his people, it is necessary to recognize the existence and work of an evil enemy. In this romance with our loving Creator, we must acknowledge the titanic, cosmic struggle between good and evil that is part of our adventure with God in this fallen world.

Satan is real. If we are seeking to know Jesus intimately and to love him with all of our hearts, if we desire to faithfully do God's will and reveal his love in the power of his Spirit, then we can be sure Satan will be working to keep us back from such a walk with God. Though Satan is only one person, through the spirit realm, he may have access to many people at once, and he has his demon hordes to help him carry out his nefarious warfare against God's people.

The enemy of our souls will tempt us to do that which is contrary to God's will. He will buffet us, lie to us, try to confuse or deceive us, try to afflict us, try to put us in bondage to things contrary to real life, try to divide us from other believers, and discourage us on our journey with God. The devil will work through an army of demons to distract us from God's plan. He will strive to destroy our trust in God and to get us to turn away from our allegiance to God and his purposes. The word Satan had as its original meaning "adversary." Of those who strive to walk with God, he truly is the adversary.

The enemy will work hard at pulling us away from our love for God—not just because he hates us, but because he so vehemently hates God. God is omnipotent, so the devil knows he can't overcome or wound God directly. But knowing God's love for his children, Satan knows the only way he can hurt God is to prevent God's children from experiencing all of the life and joy that God's love desires for them and that his amazing grace has provided for them.

When believers truly and deeply love God, trust him wholeheartedly, and stand upon his promises from the Word, the enemy loses territory in his control of the world and the lives of God's people. When God's children pray from a place of abiding in Christ and expectant faith, the enemy loses territory. When God's people obey him to carry forth the good news of his triumphant grace to this world, the enemy loses territory. The enemy knows this. Although he lost his authority by Christ's victory on the cross, he still uses lies and intimation to hold on to his territory until his final judgment.

Jesus sent out disciples to share the good news, heal and deliver those in need, and announce the kingdom of God. When they returned, they joyfully reported to Jesus how God had worked through them to heal and set people free from the bondage of Satan. Jesus responded, " ... *I saw Satan fall like lightning from heaven*" (Luke 10:18). Jesus saw the kingdom of God advancing, and Satan falling from his rulership in the lives of people as his disciples brought the good news of the kingdom of God. The Scriptures then say, "*In that hour Jesus rejoiced in the Spirit*" (Luke 10:21). The original language pictures this as exuberant joy— jumping, leaping, and spinning joy! Such is God's great love for us. He exuberantly rejoices over our deliverance from bondage to experience freedom and life in him! Satan despises such joy of God and hates such triumph of God's kingdom. He fights against it with evil passion. He opposes God's children through whom God works to bring his kingdom of love to the world.

There are several serious errors that we can commit when we consider overcoming the enemy in our lives. One mistake is to blame Satan for some of our struggles, trials, or afflictions when we are actually experiencing the consequences of our wrong or selfish choices. We can also accuse the devil when the difficulties we face are a part of our heavenly Father's loving discipline to bring us back to his plan for our lives.

Another mistake is to pay too much attention to the devil, be preoccupied with him, and be overly fearful of him and his power and the work of his demon throngs. God has provided for us, and promised us for our real experience, the defeat of the enemy in our lives so that our focus could be on seeking first the kingdom of God. However, an equally serious mistake is to ignore Satan's harmful, incapacitating influences and let him deceive us. We can err by not realizing the nature and seriousness of the spiritual struggle with evil in our hearts and the world.

When we recognize the ways of our enemy, we can prepare for his attacks. God's Word tells us, *"Be sober, be vigilant; because your adversary the devil walks about like a roaring lion, seeking whom he may devour"* (1 Pet. 5:8). Paul wrote about our serious warfare, *"we do not wrestle against flesh and blood, but against principalities, against powers, against the rulers of the darkness of this age, against spiritual hosts of wickedness"* (Eph. 6:12).

If we understand some of Satan's ways of attack, we can be better prepared to resist him. We can even turn his assaults to our advantage as we seek to love God more and more. The enemy will fight all of God's children, but he often fights in proportion to certain spiritual places in which we stand.

Satan will fight us in proportion to the closeness of our walk with God. The enemy knows that the more in-depth our intimacy with God, the more God can display his love through us, and the more his will can be done by us. The enemy is fearfully aware that the more consecrated we are to God, the more God can trust us and work through us to take the enemy's territory. Living close to God doesn't ensure the enemy will not tempt us or try to discourage us. Quite the opposite, it means the enemy may fight us all the more. God has promised to protect us under the shelter of his wings and deliver us by the mighty power of his presence. We can look to God always, trust in his completed work of Calvary, seek refuge in his presence, take courage in his promise and power, and be diligent not to give the enemy a foothold in our lives in any way. *" ... Do not give the devil a foothold"* (Eph. 4:27 NIV). Jesus once spoke of the prince of this world coming to thwart him in doing his Father's will, but the devil had nothing in Jesus, no claim upon him, no place for a foothold. (John 14:30). If we consecrate all we are to God, the devil may battle us but has no footing in our lives to trap us or defeat us.

The devil will fight us in proportion to the strategic importance of our current place of use in God's plan and kingdom. Everyone in the body of

Christ is important, but there are times when our lives and God working through us are crucial to something specific and significant that God wants to do. The enemy will try to prevent us from fulfilling this vital calling. Especially will the enemy fight in proportion to the number of people we are bringing to life in Christ or to the number of saints we are encouraging to faithfulness. Every soul saved is a tremendous loss to the enemy's plans to hold territory from God but is a huge, joyous, everlasting, God-glorifying win for the kingdom of God.

Satan will fight us in proportion to the closeness of our association with people whom God is using mightily. God desires to use all of his children mightily. But at strategic times in the advancement of his kingdom, some leaders must press through obstacles, set forth a challenge, and lead the charge into God's purposes by the guidance and power of God's Spirit. The people closely associated with God's chosen leaders are crucial to their success and the success of God's work. The enemy will fight this relationship fiercely. When a person may feel estranged from a leader, those may be the very times when the leader most needs their love and support and prayers.

The enemy will fight in proportion to the power and fruitfulness of our prayer lives. Nothing so strikes real terror in the enemy's heart as a saint upon his or her knees in prayer. Satan will do everything in his limited power to keep a person or a group of people from seeking God's face in fervent, believing, expectant, persevering prayer. The enemy knows that personal and corporate prayers release God's presence and power upon the earth to take his territory. No wonder the devil will so actively fight prayer and people who pray.

The powers of darkness will war against us in proportion to the spiritual vision that God has given us concerning what he desires to do for his glory in the world. The enemy will try to discourage us from believing and giving ourselves to what God has promised. The enemy will fight us in proportion to the greatness and importance of that God-given vision.

The devil will fight in proportion to the degree of spiritual oneness to which a group of believers aspires to experience. He knows that the spiritual unity of God's children will cause the world to believe the good news that God has sent Jesus into the world and that God truly loves them (John 17:21, 23). The longing, prayers, and lives of a group of people who are one in Christ will open the heavens upon the world in mighty, life-giving, God-glorifying power. This importance of oneness is why the enemy works so ruthlessly and relentlessly to cause division among Christians in the church, especially when believers seek true unity through absolute surrender to God's love and will.

The enemy will fight in proportion to the importance of the specific obedience just ahead of us. Sometimes there is an act of obedience just before us that is crucial to God carrying out his loving plans. If the enemy knows of this, he will fight us vigorously to keep us back from that obedience.

We can be alert to all of these ways of the enemy. If the devil is fighting us severely in one or more of these areas, it actually may be a reason for our encouragement. Each of these cases may be an indicator that God must be up to something good. The enemy's attacks may point to our growing relationship with God and his desire to involve us in his will. Satan's assault may mean that we are threatening his domain. So, we can be inspired and more determined, by God's grace and power, to resist the enemy and claim those important victories that God desires for the advancement of his kingdom.

How do we overcome the enemy? How can we respond when the enemy comes to accuse, buffet, tempt, discourage, and defeat us? We can look to God's Word to learn about those who are attacked and accused by Satan. *"And they overcame him by the blood of the Lamb and by the word of their testimony, and they did not love their lives to the death"* (Rev. 12:11).

When Christ shed his blood on Calvary, he won our victory over the enemy. By his crucifixion and resurrection, Jesus overcame the worst that sin and evil could do. Christ, the sacrificial lamb, took away Satan's authority over our lives when he redeemed us by his shed blood. Now, as we are in Christ, we can share his victory. Because of Christ's atoning work, God has forgiven us of our sins, and Satan has no proper grounds to accuse us. The devil still rages furiously against God's children because he knows his time is limited, but Christ has already accomplished his ultimate defeat.

What Christ accomplished for us includes the provision of those spiritual weapons now available to us. The Apostle Paul has written, "*Put on the whole armor of God, that you may be able to stand against the wiles of the devil. For we do not wrestle against flesh and blood, but against principalities, against powers, against the rulers of the darkness of this age, against spiritual hosts of wickedness in the heavenly places. Therefore take up the whole armor of God, that you may be able to withstand in the evil day, and having done all to stand. Stand therefore, having girded your waist with truth, having put on the breastplate of righteousness, and having shod your feet with the preparation of the gospel of peace; above all, taking the shield of faith with which you will be able to quench all the fiery darts of the wicked one. And take the helmet of salvation, and the sword of the Spirit, which is the word of God; praying always with all prayer and supplication in the Spirit*" (Eph. 6:11-18).

All these provisions for spiritual warfare are made available for us in Christ by his overwhelming victory on the cross, his resurrection, and his ascension to the right hand of the Father to ever make intercession for us. The armor of God includes the Word of God as the sword of the Holy Spirit. This Word held and declared in trust becomes our powerful offensive weapon against the powers of darkness. Christ won for us this armor of warfare, and we employ it through our faith and our praying in the Spirit. "*... Prayer is essential in this ongoing warfare*" (Eph. 6:18 The Message).

When the enemy comes to assault us with lies and accusations to keep us from loving, trusting, and obeying God, how will we respond? We could argue with him and attempt to contradict his allegations by giving a list of what we've done that is good, trying to balance out the bad. This strategy will never work or bring success. We could just give in to his attacks and give up our place of victory and spiritual usefulness to God. Or, we could respond, "Yes, I have failed. I have fallen short, but I plead the merits of the blood of Christ. I plead the blood of Jesus. I stand by grace in the presence of Christ, my righteousness. I resist you in the name of Jesus." The enemy has no winning rebuttal for such a plea. This appeal is the only plea by which we can claim the victory over the enemy.

Another vital provision that Christ won for us by the shedding of his blood was the gift of the Holy Spirit. Christ removed the barriers of sin that separated us from God so that God, the Holy Spirit, could come and dwell in our hearts. The Holy Spirit makes the work of the cross operative in our lives. The Holy Spirit enables and empowers us to resist the enemy and overcome his attacks as we genuinely surrender to his presence and authority.

The persecuted saints also overcame by the "the word of their testimony." As we boldly declare our confidence in Christ's work for us, as we share his abundant grace with others, as we confess our faith in Christ's triumph for us, the enemy is discomfited and loses his influence over us. As we declare God's Word of promise and power from a trusting heart, the enemy has no answer. In times of trial, persecution, or even martyrdom, our witness to Christ's victory can help others resist and overcome the enemy.

" ... *They were willing to give up their lives"* (Rev. 12:11 CEV). Those martyred for their faith loved God more than their fear of dying. This passage of Scripture also points us to one of the central truths of the full gospel. Jesus presented this truth many times as one of the keys to our deepest victories: "*For whoever desires to save his life will lose it, but whoever loses his life for My sake and the gospel's will save it*" (Mark 8:35).

If we give everything in our lives to Christ, if we are his entirely, if we have put Christ on the throne of our hearts by the Holy Spirit, the enemy finds little ground in our hearts for his deceits. The enemy will still fight us furiously, but if we genuinely lose our lives for Christ's sake, then we will find overcoming life. We will defeat the enemy through Christ's work and the Holy Spirit's power. We can give ourselves entirely to God's purposes and lose our lives in Christ at every moment of spiritual attack and every place of conscious choice. God will meet us at these times and these places with overcoming grace.

If we sincerely desire to know God intimately and love him with all of our hearts, the enemy will soon confront us. We must not give in to the enemy. There is too much at stake for us and those we could reach for Christ. By Christ's presence and provision, we will overcome. The joyous, fruitful life in communion with Christ is worth the fight.

God will even use the enemy's attacks to strengthen our faith and our resolve to love him supremely. God will use the times of resisted temptation to prepare us for more significant victories ahead. We can overcome the enemy. Christ has already won our victory for us. God will take us through the enemy's fight to greater depths of communion with him, greater portrayals of his love, and greater accomplishments of his will all for his glory.

Chapter 19

Living in the Fullness of the Spirit

The Christian life can only be lived by the presence and power of the Holy Spirit within us. If we desire to know God intimately, if we long to love him passionately, this will be possible only because of the Holy Spirit's gracious and miraculous work. Although we have a choice whether we will respond, God's grace and call always precede our choice. May we never get over the marvel and immensity of God's grace toward us! This grace reaches to where we are to envelop us in the embrace of divine love and bring us to God's purposes for our lives.

The amazing grace of God is in operation when the Holy Spirit convicts us, calls us, and draws us to God. The Holy Spirit then opens to us the wonder and efficacy of Christ's redeeming grace. The Holy Spirit applies the atoning work of Christ's crucifixion in our forgiveness. The Spirit of God does the work of regeneration in our spirits, making us a new creation in Christ. Our innermost person had become separated from God by Adam's sin and our own choices. Separation from God is spiritual death, for God is the source of all spiritual life. The sacrificial death of Jesus on the cross removed the barriers between God and us so that God could reconcile us to him. We were brought home to God and the rapturous fellowship of his love.

We experience the new birth as the Holy Spirit comes within us and quickens our spirit to come alive and alert to God once again. The Holy Spirit then takes up sacred residence within our spirits. In this way, our spiritual life begins as a Christian, and we are brought into blissful communion with God by the life and power of the Holy Spirit's indwelling presence.

This life of walking in the fullness of the Spirit is a life of trust and obedience. It is not seeking great things for ourselves. It is just seeking God himself and trusting him as a child. Walking in the Spirit is a leaning upon God minute by minute, communing with his Holy Spirit, worshiping in his presence, walking in his love, resting in his promise, following in his guidance, witnessing in his power, serving in his gifting, and joying in his grace. The greatness of this privilege is beyond what our minds can fully comprehend, our hearts can grasp, or our words can express. This experience is the ultimate fulfillment for our lives, the greatest desire and pleasure of God, and the grand purpose of all creation. By our lives lived from this place of God's indwelling presence, we reveal his love to the world in saving grace.

By the Holy Spirit, the life of the indwelling Christ works through our individual, unique personalities as we say yes to His Lordship. The Holy Spirit in us is what makes us alive in Christ. Our daily walk with God—knowing him, loving him, and obeying him—is by the Holy Spirit's life and work. Christ's love is in us and through us by the Holy Spirit. " ...*The love of God has been poured in our hearts by the Holy Spirit*" (Rom. 5:5). As we allow him, the Holy Spirit brings us to Christlikeness and the fruit of his holy presence working in our lives: *"love, joy, peace, longsuffering, kindness, goodness, faithfulness, gentleness, and self-control"* (Gal. 5:22-23).

The Holy Spirit strengthens us. The Holy Spirit makes the Word of God a revelation to our hearts and makes real our communion with God. God's Holy Spirit guides us by the written Word and leads us personally and specifically in our lives each day. The Holy Spirit empowers us to do God's will, resist the devil, and with divine love, witness to others concerning the wonder and power of God's saving grace. The Holy Spirit bestows upon us gifts so we can fulfill our part in the body of Christ. The Holy Spirit empowers us to overcome the flesh, to take our carnal nature daily to the cross of Christ as we deny ourselves by his power. The Holy Spirit imputes and imparts to us the righteousness of Christ. With the help of the Holy Spirit, we can endure hardships, affliction, and persecution. The third person of the Trinity assists us in prayer. Genuine prayer is the Holy Spirit praying through us. The Spirit anoints us to live our lives with supernatural impact. We need, we must have, the Holy Spirit to fulfill the purposes of God. Without the Holy Spirit's work in our lives, we live with only human strength with human impact, but with the Holy Spirit, we can have supernatural power with eternal fruit.

Jesus was physically present with his disciples when he walked the earth. Because of the work of Christ to remove the barrier between God and us, Jesus can now be within us by the Holy Spirit. What a wonder of God's divine love and mercy! Oh, that our hearts could grasp that God passionately desires to have such personal communion with his children!

What affection we should have for the Holy Spirit who brings us into communion with the Godhead! What sweet but passionate devotion to the One who loves us with a boundless, breathtaking love! What desire to open every part of our hearts to his precious and holy indwelling! What longing for his presence in our every thought and action! What deep commitment to his love! What complete trust in his control, direction, and enabling power for our lives! Here is our fulfillment! Here is our real living! Here is participation in the very purposes of God! It is joy unspeakable and full of glory!

May we never take lightly or ignore such an indescribably wonder-filled gift as God's Holy Spirit. Who are we that God would create us to be his temple, the dwelling place of his holy, loving presence? The omnipotent Creator offers us his very self in the Holy Spirit to live in our hearts that we might experience and express his unfailing love.

Yet, many try to live the full Christian life without this intimate relationship with the Holy Spirit. They attempt the miraculous in their strength. It cannot be done. The Christian life is a supernatural life of God living in us. God lives through our unique personalities by the indwelling presence of the Holy Spirit. This indwelling presence is the most astonishing offer that God could ever make.

Why do many Christians not live in the fullness and the power of this matchless gift? Some may reject this truth because it doesn't match their own experience. But we dare not measure reality by only our own limited or handicapped experiences. Doesn't God's Word speak about this full Christian experience? From past centuries to the present, many saints can testify to the reality and fruitfulness of this immeasurable blessing.

Some may be frightened from this experience of living in the Spirit's fullness because of the strange, unbiblical way some people behave when claiming this blessing from God. The counterfeit should not keep us away from the real. Whatever other signs may accompany such a fullness of

God's Holy Spirit, the most excellent evidence of God's indwelling will always be the divine love of God that flows through us to others in mighty rivers of grace as we live in Christlikeness.

Some may reject this abundant Christian life because they realize that it calls for the complete surrender of their lives to God. Yet, only in full consecration is full freedom and fulfillment and the abundant life Christ came to offer us.

Others may not have realized or understood that such a life in fellowship with the Holy Spirit is possible. God in his Word invites us to such a blessing (Luke 11:13; John 7:35-37; Acts 1:8; 4:23-31; Rom. 8:1-17; Gal. 5:16-25; Eph. 5:18). God calls us to live in an ever-growing fullness of the Spirit's fellowship and influence.

Some may not claim this position in Christ, this real experience of the Holy Spirit's work, because of their adherence to narrow theological prescriptions. We can doctrinally split hairs with our definitions and explanations and not appreciate or appropriate God's full work in our lives. When dear, hungry, child-like souls cry out for more of God's Holy Spirit, they are asking for the Holy Spirit to be more real in fellowship, more influential in guidance, more powerfully revealed in their lives. Some would say that we can't ask to be filled with the Spirit (although God's Word describes it this way) because we received all of the Holy Spirit as a person at conversion. That's true, but the Holy Spirit may not be fully in control of our lives or fully manifested through us. Would it not be more important to have the real experience of the Holy Spirit's manifested presence and power in child-like faith than to exclude it from our experience by our technical definitions? I would rather have a real hunger for the Holy Spirit's manifested presence, and the actual experience of his love and power working in my life than just to be able to describe it theologically. We can miss God's richest blessing and cause others to miss it because God's gracious work doesn't fit into our traditions or preconceived ideas.

Could it be that some like to cling to certain hair-splitting definitions to hide their lack of experience of the Spirit's fullness in their lives? God's children have been divided too long, too deeply by nitpicking judgments of others' experience when the world awaits a demonstration of God's real presence and love in those who call themselves Christians. We need not argue over our terms. Let's just encourage one another to a more life-changing, biblically promoted, God-glorifying experience of the Holy Spirit's work. I don't care what you call it. We need it. God offers this amazing Holy Spirit-blessed life—this wondrous, intimate relationship with himself.

What do we mean when we say that we need the Holy Spirit's power to operate in our Christian lives? What are we talking about when we say we need God's power? We are talking about the spiritual power that is great enough to produce great saints again. We are talking about the spiritual anointing that gives heavenly power and glorious freedom in our worship. We are talking about a great mystery, an awe-inspiring quality that marks the church as divine and not earthly. It is something remarkable, fearsome, breathtaking, and amazing. It is something that causes the world to stand in astonishment of the mystery and wonder of God. We are talking about a divine love that flows through God's children like a mighty torrent to those around them in this wounded world. We are talking about an illuminating power that lifts us to a heavenly vision to see as God sees and to understand what matters in the purposes of God. We are talking about a power that fills our hearts with an enormous and relentless passion for sharing Christ with others. We are talking about the mighty power that enables the church to push back the darkness, overcome all obstacles and spiritual foes, and take a stand in a place of loving certainty. We are talking about the divine life that produces spiritual fruit in lasting abundance. We are talking about the divine power that convicts our hearts of sin and shows us our need for God. We are talking about a person—not a mechanical, impersonal force—but a person—God himself! We open ourselves to a person who, with loving, limitless power, can do all things. We are talking about the power of the Holy Spirit.

We will have as much spiritual success and eternal, God-glorifying fruit in our lives as we have of the Holy Spirit in us and through us manifesting his presence. The world doesn't need a new definition of the gospel for it to be relevant. The world needs a real and fresh demonstration of its power. The desire and cry of hearts that hunger for

God himself is that they might know the Holy Spirit in ever greater fullness and power so that God may accomplish his will through them for the honor of his name.

The indwelling Holy Spirit transformed the lives of the early Christians. The disciples were changed from timid, fearful, vacillating, doubt-filled, divisive, petty, self-centered followers to dynamic, loving, confident, courageous, miracle-experiencing witnesses for Christ. This same transforming power is available and promised for our lives.

How do we walk in this way of the fullness of the Spirit in our lives? This walk begins and continues with our hunger for God himself. When we are born from above by the Holy Spirit because of our faith in Christ's work on the cross, the Holy Spirit takes up his dwelling place in our spirits. Within us, the Holy Spirit desires to reign with Christ on the throne of our hearts, enlivening and empowering us by his presence. After conversion, God calls us to grow continually and daily in the manifestations of the Holy Spirit's work and influence in our lives. (How sad that many Christians do not grow into the wonder-filled experience of all God desires to do through them. What does that mean for God's work in the world?)

We grow daily in the Holy Spirit's influence and power in our lives as we feed on God's Word, spend time communing with him in fervent prayer, deny self, and obey the Holy Spirit's promptings. We grow as we love those around us with Christ's love, witness to others about the good news, and in child-like faith believe God's promise for Holy Spirit's work.

In addition to the day-by-day growth in the Spirit, many of God's servants have crisis experiences when the Holy Spirit does a mighty work of grace in the soul. Many God-blessed and God-used Christians testify that they have progressed in the Holy Spirit's blessing for them by times of an extraordinary experience of God's purifying, delivering, and empowering work. At certain times God's children have realized their great need and their complete inadequacy to fulfill God's call effectively on their own. They hunger and thirst for more of God himself, for a deeper fellowship with him, for more of his work in their lives, for more of his power to fulfill his purposes. Such was the experience of the apostles even after their initial filling by the Holy Spirit at Pentecost (Acts 4:23-31).

God meets the hungry heart who comes in desperation and expectant faith. He meets them with a greater revelation of himself and impartation of his glory. God reveals himself to desperate men and women who seek his face and stand upon his promises in expectant faith. There may be one or more of these special times of crisis and blessing in a person's life when he or she grows in God's grace and is prepared to be used in a more significant way for God and his glory. May we hunger for all God has for us!

We maintain our victory and our place of Holy Spirit enduement by our love disciplines of faith, obedience to God's Word and Spirit, worship, and our serving and witnessing. However, in living in the fullness of the Spirit, we cannot coast or maintain a non-growing place for long. We will either be advancing or retreating. We either respond to God's call to come higher in his purposes and more rooted in his love, or we fall back from our most intimate communion with God. We will continue to grow in a relationship with the Holy Spirit according to the level of our faith, humility, obedience, love, and our ravishing hunger for God. God is with us always, wooing us onward into his love and blessings, and he enables us every step of the way by the operation of his amazing grace.

We must guard the living sacrifice of ourselves that we take to the altar of our hearts. We must shew away birds of prey that come to take our offering of ourselves to God. As Abraham guarded the sacrifice that signified his covenant with God (Gen. 15:11), we must shew away the vultures of prey that will come to steal our sacrifice from the altar of our devotion to God. I assure you the birds will come. We must drive away vultures of pride, negligence, self-pity, bitterness, the lust of the flesh, earthly cares, doubt, fear, and demonic accusations. The very God who calls us to lose our lives to find them will enable us to keep the sacrifice before him.

Christ gave himself as the supreme sacrifice so we could live the life of the Spirit. We meet God at the altar of our hearts, where we receive by grace the work and blessing of his Holy Spirit. If we go in faith and love to encounter God daily at that altar, God will meet us and send the fire of his Holy Spirit to our open and fire-hungry hearts. May God set our hearts ablaze with his presence and love for the glory of his name!

This beautiful gift of God's indwelling presence operating in our lives is offered to us. One of the greatest calamities of the church and the lives of Christians is that such a blessing is available and unclaimed. One of the main reasons for the church's little impact in the world is the lack of the Holy Spirit's divine power and his overflowing divine love in the lives of Christians.

The serious and continual danger is that we would be content with something less than what God intended for us—that we would be satisfied with less than what Christ offers us that came at such a cost to him. We cannot be content with less than the ever-growing fullness of the Holy Spirit in our lives. The needs around us are enormous. The world is full of hopeless, hurting, and broken people. People are missing eternal life in Christ. Millions are going into eternity apart from God's love. God is so little glorified and, yet, he is worthy of so much honor. Only God's people overflowing with his presence, power, and love by the Holy Spirit can have a real and eternal impact on this world. If there ever was a time we needed to live in the Spirit's fullness, it is now.

God is looking for a person or group of people who hunger and thirst for the fullness of his indwelling presence and long for him to work in this world. God is searching for those he can fill and overflow with the glory of his presence. God will manifest himself to the measure of the emptiness and thirst with which we come to him. If we come to him with a thimble, we will get a thimbleful. If we come to him with a bucket, we will get a bucketful. If we come to him with a 100-gallon barrel, we will get a barrelful. With what expectation and thirst do we come to God?

A servant of God, much used in England and around the world, came to America. While preaching in New York, he visited Niagara Falls. Friends who were with him have reported that as he stood by those mighty waters pouring over the falls, he lifted his face to heaven, and with tears running down his cheeks, he prayed, "Like that, Lord, like that in me! Out of my innermost being let there flow like this vast rivers of living water." We can cry out like this in longing for the work of God's Holy Spirit through our lives for the honor of his name. May God give us desperate, hungry, and thirsty hearts! Oh, how much we need the Spirit to flow in mighty rivers into the world.

On the last and great day of the Feast of Tabernacles, Jesus stood and cried out, saying, " ... *If anyone thirsts, let him come to Me and drink. He who believes in Me, as the Scripture has said, out of his heart* (innermost being) *will flow rivers of living water! But this He spoke concerning the Spirit"* (John 7:37- 39). Like this, Lord, like this! Like this in rivers of living water through my life, through our lives to the world.

So Longs My Soul

Chapter 20

Heart-Cry for Revival

Do our hearts hunger and thirst for the living God? Do we genuinely desire to know God in intimate fellowship? To love him, supremely? To live in ways that are pleasing to him? To live lives that lift him and glorify him? If we do, we will want our hearts to be in tune with his heart. We will aspire to love what he loves. We will desire our hearts to break with what breaks his heart and our lives to celebrate what brings him joy.

God's heart is that those he created to walk with him would accept the embrace of his love. Christ's love-saturated desire is that those for whom he was crucified would come to him for an abundant life. Our heavenly Father longs with an immeasurable, immutable love that those he made in his image would open their hearts to his saving grace. God is seeking those who will be passionate about that for which he is passionate.

As we look around us, we see that God's loving desires for this world are not being satisfied. The need is great. People are empty, confused, and hurting—looking frantically for something to fill their lives—something to make sense of living. Many people are stumbling through their lives without hope. Most people are trying to fill their lives with things other than God that will not satisfy them. People have no moral compass, no solid ground on which to stand to evaluate what matters. What is good is called evil, and what is evil is called good. Marriage is trivialized, and the crucially important family unit is disintegrating. Unbridled lust and perversity define our culture, and hatred between groups increases. In this sin-fractured and wounded world, multitudes of people are missing the abundant life in Christ. Millions of people die each week missing their God-desired destiny, heading for a catastrophic calamity—the tragedy of everlasting separation from God.

With all of this need, the sad truth is that the church no longer has much impact on the world. She displays too little of God's holiness, too little of the love of Christ, and too little of God's Holy Spirit power in her witness of the good news. That which has no life cannot bring life to the world.

Our God is a God of amazing, self-sacrificial love. He has stepped into our world to offer us his love and eternal life. We look around at those God loves in this world and see multitudes missing the life he offers. We observe the church missing her divine calling to bring life to the world. We see our God not receiving the love, glory, and honor for which he is so infinitely worthy. Shouldn't our hearts break in sorrow? Shouldn't we have a passionate longing for God to be worthily worshipped and adored? Shouldn't our response be to cry out to God for a mighty work of his grace and power in his lifeless church and this heart-wounded world?

Ours is not the only time when things seemed dark or difficult for God's church or for God's cause of redeeming love. There have been times when society's moral condition was malignant, and people cared little about seeking or glorifying God. The church was without contagious life and seemed powerless to make any difference in the world. At such times, God has moved in divine intervention in our world with a Holy Spirit invasion from heaven. He has sent wonderful, powerful times of his refreshing, reviving work for the church, and a great harvest of people were born again into the newness of life. God has worked in such miraculous, remarkable ways that the moral condition of whole nations was elevated to righteousness. God has done it before. He can do it again. Such a powerful, astonishing work of God's grace is once again what we desperately need.

The only answer for the great need in the church and the world is God himself. Our hope is not in government or economics or advanced education. Our hope is in God and his working in the hearts and lives of people. Our feeble human attempts with only human resources will never be sufficient. We need a mighty, miraculous work of God from heaven. We need God to do what only he can do.

We must not try to bring revival by our professionalism, propaganda, or fleshly promotions. Revival can only come by God's spirit. The presence of spiritual hunger, the prevailing of prayer, the loving proclamation of the good news, and the pre-eminence of the Holy Spirit in all things allow God to bring the world-changing, spiritual revival that we need.

Our purely human endeavors to meet the depth and seriousness of the need we face is like putting Band-Aids on cancer. We need more. As Jeremiah put it, we must do more than *"offer superficial treatments for my people's mortal wound"* (Jer. 6:14 NLT). The greatest need of America and the world is a Christ-lifting, devil-defeating, heart-transforming, God-sent revival!

On his way to see King Ahab during a severe drought in Israel, Elijah encountered Obadiah. The king had sent Obadiah to find even a little grass during the drought-caused famine. This can be like so many of our churches. They see the need, see the famine, but they are trying to bring relief by looking for leftover, dried up grass for a temporary earthly fix. What we need is rain from heaven! We need showers of blessing to end the drought and famine. We can be out looking for dried-up grass when we ought to be looking for heavenly rain.

Too often in church, too many meetings can just be explained in natural ways. We meet, pray, sing, have a little program, and maybe get a bit of emotional lift. We need meetings with the work of God that can't be explained by natural means—that can be explained only by a supernatural breaking through of God himself.

I have attended many church growth conferences where well-known experts on leadership have given principles for a church to grow: information on brochures, greeters, music that attracts, layperson follow-ups, identifying needs in the community, developing programs and taking actions to meet those needs, visual attractiveness and comfort of facilities, etc. All of these things are good and important for helping a church to function better. But the local Kiwanis or Lion's Club could do all of these things. You could do all of this without the Holy Spirit and grow a big church. But where's the divine dimension? My disappointment is that we can say little about repentance, prayer, brokenness, or the awfulness of sin in the church that blocks God's work. Too often, we don't consider sufficiently God's grace and power that release the divine life and growth we need. Common to all great moves of God has been an awesome sense of God's holiness, an overwhelming conviction of sin, a heart-stirring revelation of God's love and grace, desperate hunger for God himself, and a great desire for God to receive glory.

We need and must have a revival of God's life in the church and a mighty awakening in the world to God's saving grace. We must genuinely know that we need God desperately and have in our hearts a deep, honest, earnest cry for revival. Only God's power is sufficient to change our hearts and transform our world. Only his love will win, and only his glorious presence can prevail. My heart's cry is for such an amazing work of divine glory.

What is revival? Jonathan Edwards wrote, during the First Great Awakening in America, "God hath had it much on His heart, from all eternity, to glorify His dear and only begotten Son; and there are some special seasons that He appoints to that end, wherein He comes forth with omnipotent power to fulfill His promise and oath to Him: and these times are times of remarkable pouring out of His Spirit, to advance His kingdom; such a day is a day of His power." (From the Works of Jonathan Edwards as quoted, "In the Day of Thy Power," by Arthur Wallis, Christian Literature Crusade, 1956)

Spiritual revival is the divine intervention of God into the world and the lives and affairs of men and women. Revival is God revealing himself in awesome holiness and irresistible love and power. It is a mighty manifestation of God's presence, bringing life to the church, transforming lives, and spilling over in a flood of saving grace. When God moves, heaven opens upon Christians, and the manifest presence of God flows through the church, through the lives of his children to bring the lost to Christ. Revival is first a reviving of God's people to abundant, overflowing life. Then, this divine life is revealed and expressed in power through the church to the world, and the Holy Spirit awakens people to the call of Christ. When this happens on the large scale we need, there is a great awakening of people to God's abundant life, and cultures and nations are changed.

Revival is God's manifested presence to and through his people. Theologians have a way of speaking about the presence of God. There is God's *general presence*—God is God in his omnipresence. He is everywhere present. Then, there is the *personal presence* of God when

God comes into each of our spirits personally at our new birth. But there is also God's *manifest presence* when God's presence breaks through from the supernatural realm into the natural realm upon his people in glory. We need God's manifest presence to break through upon Christians, the church, and the world in life-changing power.

Isaiah cries out, *"Oh, that You would rend the heavens! That You would come down! That the mountains might shake at Your presence—as fire burns brushwood, as fire causes water to boil—to make Your name known"* (Isa. 64:1-2). These words were Isaiah's prophetic cry on behalf of the children of Israel, but it is also a cry for all of God's children for all times for God's mighty work in this world. May it not also be our cry?

What is the purpose of revival? We want revival not just to eliminate problems in our church. (If a Holy Spirit revival breaks out, there may be bigger problems of a whole different type as uncommitted people are opposed to it and as the kingdom of God challenges the kingdom of this world.) We want revival not just to validate our ministries or pack our pews or fill our offering plates. We want revival for the reason God desires this astounding work of his grace. We desire revival so the bride of Christ can be complete. The preparation of a bride for Christ is the purpose of the universe. We long for revival so that people of this world who are dearly loved by God could be reached and reborn into eternal fellowship with him. Jesus said, *"the Son of Man has come to seek and to save that which was lost"* (Luke 19:10). We want Jesus to be lifted to the world in wonder, love, and power to draw people to himself and his saving grace (John 12:32). We hunger for revival so that God's children might have abundant life and live out a present demonstration of the kingdom of God on earth. Jesus taught us to pray, *"Your kingdom come. Your will be done on earth as it is in heaven"* (Matt. 6:10).

However, the main reason we should desire for God to work in revival is so that he will be exalted and glorified. The deeper truth is that it's not just revival we seek, but it is first of all the glory of the Reviver. It's about God. It's about glorifying God. It's about God at the center of it all. If it is not about God's glory, it is not a real, heaven-sent revival. We want God to be worshipped, adored, and honored in an intimate relationship with his church for whom he gave his life. When we delight in God, know him personally, and live the way of God's kingdom, we are fulfilled, and God is glorified. The Lamb of God deserves the reward of his love and suffering. Worthy is the Lamb who was slain to receive all glory, honor, and praise!

You may say that God doesn't work by way of revival anymore, but God has always desired his people to be fully alive in his presence and reveal his glory to the world. God still works by way of a supernatural reviving of his people to awaken this world. In biblical accounts and through history since Bible times, we see God working to restore his people to intimacy with himself, to obedience to his will, and to be a light to the nations.

Although God works in variety and ever-surprising ways, we see a repetition of his manner of working in the history of his people. God's children are prone to turn away from him. Yet, because of God's compassion to call us back to him, we see a pattern in the manifestation of God's moving in revival. We see God's work to bring a group of people into intimate relationships with him and, then, through them, reach to redeem a lost world. But then, sadly, God's people turn away from him to find their delight and their purpose for living in other things than him. *"For my people have committed two evils: They have forsaken Me, the fountain of living waters, and hewn themselves cisterns—broken cisterns that can hold no water"* (Jer. 2:13). God calls his people to repent and return to his love and his ways. If people do not respond, God may send discipline or judgment as an act of love to bring them back to himself. If people do respond and cry for help, God will come again to his people in a powerful manifestation of his presence and love. God (Jesus) is exalted, and he mightily draws the lost to saving faith in him.

We see this pattern revealed over and over again in the Old Testament. This way of God's work occurred in the time of Asa, Jehoash, Hezekiah, Josiah, Zerubbabel, and Nehemiah. We hear a cry for this work of reviving in Psalms, Isaiah, Jeremiah, and elsewhere in God's Word. We also repeatedly find the promises of God to hear the cries of his people. As described in the New Testament, the outpouring of God's Holy Spirit on the day of Pentecost was the most potent coming of God's life to his people that the world has ever experienced.

Since biblical times we have seen the pattern repeated many times in history. God's people turn to him in broken-hearted repentance. They cry out to God that he might again manifest himself, and that a great harvest of people would come to find eternal life in him. And we see over and over God responding to that cry with a mighty working of his Holy Spirit.

We observe the current moral condition of the general culture around us. We see the lifelessness of much of the church and her powerlessness to impact the world. We are aware that millions around us are living without an abundant life of fellowship with God. Multitudes are dying without God to languish eternally apart from him. Satisfaction with things as they are must surely be one of the greatest enemies of the working of God in the church and the world. We must not be satisfied with things as they are. We must see that God desires and promises more for those who seek him.

If we tune our hearts to God's heart in intimate fellowship, then we must feel a portion of his sorrow over those who are missing his life. We see our God, who is imminently worthy of love, worship, and honor, being rejected and forgotten. How can we not long for that which God longs—to bring his life and present spiritual kingdom through the church to this world in a display of his love and glory? How can we not passionately long for a great move of God's Holy Spirit so that God might be worshipped and honored? How can we not see it is time for God to move again in a great revival and spiritual awakening in the world?

Jesus said, *"I came to send fire on the earth"* (Luke 12:49). I believe he was speaking, not just of the fire of judgment, but was also declaring his desire for the fire of heaven, of the Holy Spirit, to come and set the world ablaze with God's love. John the Baptist said of Jesus, " *...He will baptize you with the Holy Spirit and fire*" (Luke 3:16). The fire of his Holy Spirit will judge and consume what is false and bring the real and the eternal. May God send the fire of his presence in a revival once again! May he ignite his children's hearts with a holy flame of love for Christ, his church, and those without God in the world! May the earth be set ablaze with the powerful working of our Holy and loving God!

This is my heart-cry. This must be the heart-cry of everyone who intimately loves and knows our God. Let's cry to our heavenly Father, to our God of unfailing love and abundant mercies that he would once again send a mighty revelation of his life and grace to his church and this world.

Let's prepare our hearts to receive this needed and glorious work of his love. Let's pray. Let's believe. Let's watch and witness and serve and obey and prepare in expectation. Let's see God work once again in power for the glory of his name.

Chapter 21

A River from a Rock

God works in ways of committed and continual reaching for his people. The Bible and history reveal a pattern of God's working to fulfill his purposes in the world through spiritual revival. There is not only a pattern in the way God has worked out his purposes in the world, but there is also a spiritual preparation of God's people that must take place before God can work in the fullness of his presence and power.

God is omnipotent, and he is sovereign. He is not a puppet on our strings to move by our manipulation. But he does respond to his children in line with his love and divine purposes. God will not give himself in his manifest presence to those who are not thirsty for him and those who are not open to receive him. God desires to be desired. God will reveal himself to a person or a group of people who hunger with a ravishing hunger for his presence and his glory.

God comes in manifest presence to his people when they tune their hearts to his heart, Word, and Holy Spirit—when they see through God's eyes and feel with God's heart the great need of the world. When believers are brokenhearted over their sins and lack of purity, their coldness toward God, and their lack of concern for those living without God, they are preparing for God to send revival to the church and spiritual awakening to the nations. When people are alarmed and remorseful about the church's lack of life, showers of blessing may be coming soon. When Christians are disturbed about their loved ones and millions in the world who are dying without knowing Christ's life, revival may be drawing near. When God's children are moved overwhelmingly about how their heavenly Father is so little loved and acknowledged, God may be getting ready to break through into this world with a revelation of his glory. When the spirit of prayer comes upon God's people to cry out to God, preparation for God's reviving work in the world has begun. When believers stop bickering and backbiting over nonessentials and go to their knees in brokenhearted, believing prayer, God may be getting ready to rend the heavens and come down in power.

We read this preparation guide in God's Word: "*break up your fallow ground, for it is time to seek the Lord, till He comes and rains righteousness on you*" (Hosea 10:12). Fallow ground is hard, weed-filled ground that may have yielded an abundant harvest in the past but now is unproductive for lack of cultivation. Our hearts can be unaffected by the destiny of people without God and impervious to God's daily call. Revival preparation is a time when our hardened hearts are plowed up and broken up by the work of the cross of Christ, the Word of God, and the Holy Spirit. It is a time when we remove the weeds, thorns, and thistles of sin in preparation for a fruitful harvest for a holy God. To break up the fallow ground of our hearts means to bring our hearts to a humble and contrite state of tenderness before our God. These are the only conditions of hearts that God can revive.

This brokenness brings God's people to their knees in a cry for God's mercy and his help from heaven, for only God can push back the darkness in our land, and only God can meet the depth of human need. There is a cry from the heart, "*Oh, that You would rend the heavens! That You would come down!*" (Isa. 64:1). In preparation for a great move of God, there is a claiming of God's promises in prayer for God's glory. There has never been a great and lasting revival that was not birthed and maintained by fervent, persistent, expectant prayer. It is a sign that God desires to work in a unique way when he puts a spirit of prayer upon his people. When God's people cry out in hunger, desperation, and faith from a place of true spiritual oneness with one another, then God will respond.

Sometimes this cry to God may begin with just a few spiritually hungry pilgrims praying, but then this moves others to pray. This cry reaches the heart of God, and the heavens open in a glorious work of the Holy Spirit that revives the church and brings saving life to many. The very moral level of entire communities and nations are affected in true revival and awakening.

Looking to God for revival is not a way to avoid our call to love and obedience until a move of God comes. Our diligence in the daily disciplines of our walk with God now and our loving faithfulness to share our faith with others are essential parts of the preparation that will open an expanded work of God. We are to do all that God has commanded us to do until revival comes. If we aren't passionate followers of Christ now and if we aren't faithfully and lovingly bearing witness to others now of the good news of the life in Christ, how can we expect God to trust us with that more excellent working of his Holy Spirit for which we long?

God has given many promises that he will answer us when we call to him for those things already on his heart. His promise is still trustworthy that he *"will pour water on him who is thirsty, and floods on the dry ground"* (Isa. 44:3). And though God gave a promise to Solomon for the children of Israel, the promise is still true for God's children today: *"if My people who are called by My name will humble themselves, and pray and seek My face, and turn from their wicked ways, then I will hear from heaven, and will forgive their sin and heal their land"* (2 Chron. 7:14). Continually in his Word, God has promised his people that he will respond to their cries for help. We see examples in God's Word and in history of how God has answered his people's prayers in amazing works of his grace and love.

God has the power to perform what he has promised. Since Bible times, whenever people have turned their hearts to God in hunger and repentance, God has moved in powerful ways to bring his children home to his embrace and bring honor to his name.

Just such a time of God's amazing work took place in the 1730s and 1740s and has been called the First Great Awakening. Before God sent this reviving work, America's moral and spiritual state was one of terrible degradation. Deism was becoming dominant. Atheism was on the rise. Drunkenness, debauchery, lawlessness, disregard for the value of life, and disinterest or lukewarmness in the churches were the order of the day. Under the ministry of Jonathan Edwards and other godly men, God released the Holy Spirit in a mighty revival in America. God worked in such conviction of sin and radical conversion of lives through his grace that whole communities and then nations were transformed. The social and moral atmosphere changed to a real display of love, lawfulness, and godliness.

A Second Great Awakening took place from the late 18th century through the early 19th century. After the American Revolution, once again, there had been a turning away from God and trust in his Word. Earnest prayer was made. God began to work in universities that once were Christian but which had become secularized. God did a genuine revival work to turn the nation back to God. The awakening reached the American Frontier, where an astounding move of God took place.

In the 1850s, America experienced what has been called the "Prayer Revival." Jeremiah Lamphier, a forty-six-year-old businessman, started a prayer meeting during the lunch hour at a place on Fulton Street in New York City. The first week only six people came. But the next week, there were twenty. Within six months, 10,000 businessmen were gathering for prayer in New York City. At the same time, prayer meetings were arising across America. Suddenly a great revival broke out. At times a cloud of the heavenly influence of God's Holy Spirit seemed to hang over many communities and parts of our nation. This cloud of God's manifest presence extended out miles from the American coast. People on board approaching ships became convicted and began to pray. One ship after another arrived, telling of an awesome sense of God's presence that would come over passengers and crew as they neared the American Coast. From one ship, the captain signaled a message, "Send a minister!" Another vessel, a commercial vessel, entered the port with every member of the crew converted. All of this took place without any promotion from the coast or even knowing what was happening in America. The Battleship North Carolina became a center of revival. Revival fires were kindled on many naval vessels.

At the height of the Prayer Revival, someone estimated 50,000 people a week were born into a new life in Christ. During the entire period of God's mighty work, at least 500,000 were converted in America to dynamic faith and as many as 1,000,000 worldwide. With this revival also came the rise of new social concerns and calls for social justice. The missionary movement and the roots of the abolition of slavery came as a result of the revival. The church began again to have an impact on society.

In 1904, a great revival broke out in Wales. Some of God's children had a longing for a fresh move of God's Holy Spirit. People had become indifferent to religion. Church attendance was declining, and churches were formal and lifeless. God began to work in several places in Wales, but he used a young man named Evan Roberts in a dynamic way. Evan had worked in the coal mines of Wales, but he had a heavy burden for a real move of God. Evan had prayed for a mighty, spiritual revival for thirteen years. While still a young man, with his heart aflame, he preached to a group of young people at a Monday night prayer service. They continued to meet together in hunger and anticipation. God began to work. Conviction increased. People were dramatically saved. The revival spread throughout the country. At the end of the first six months, more than 100,000 people had experienced a spiritual conversion. Communities were changed. Crime dramatically dropped. The police had nothing to do. People paid old debts and made restitution for theft and wrongdoing. There was a work slowdown in the mines because the work mules had to learn a new, non-cussing language of the miners. The moving of God's Holy Spirit spread as God worked in powerful revivals in nations worldwide.

The Hebrides off the coast of Scotland experienced an amazing revival in 1949. The spirit of God worked so powerfully that in one meeting, the minister, Duncan Campbell, had to stop preaching because he couldn't be heard over the wails of those crying out in distress under the weight of their conviction of sin. Whole areas seemed saturated in the presence of God. People fell to their knees and made God the Lord of their lives, not just in churches but also in homes, barns, fields, and along roadsides.

Other notable revivals include the Moravian revival, which began in 1720 and significantly impacted the life and ministry of John Wesley. There were great revivals in many nations around the world as a result of the work of God's Holy Spirit spreading from the 1904 awakening in Wales. Astonishing revivals broke out at Asbury College in Wilmore, Kentucky, in the early 1900s and again in 1950 and 1970. There were revivals in Shantung, China in 1927, in East Africa in the1950s, and in portions of South America in the 1970s.

Common to the great revivals have been an honoring of God's Word, an awe-filled sense of the holiness of God, an overwhelming conviction of sin, a revelation of the greatness of God's love and grace in forgiveness and regeneration, hunger for God himself, and a great desire to glorify God's name.

Our nation and the world are again in a time of moral and spiritual decay. Hearts seem much hardened to the gospel, and many churches are lifeless, loveless, and powerless. Is a spiritual revival possible in our day? Are the obstacles too large for God to overcome? Can the world ever be awakened to the love of God again? Yes, there can be another mighty spiritual awakening! Our hope is in the love, grace, power, and promises of God. It has often been that God has worked in the most dynamic, world-changing ways in the very times of the greatest darkness and spiritual decay. In deep darkness, the light of the gospel stands out all the brighter. Nothing is impossible to God. God is able, and God is longing to work in revival again.

The beginning of the eighteenth century was a time of great moral and spiritual darkness, political unrest, and social injustice in England and other parts of the world. People rejected the authority of the Bible. Religion had no spiritual power and was viewed with disdain by many. Most of the population was untouched by the church, and most of the clergies opposed salvation by faith and lived ungodly lives. Many of the political leaders were unbelievers and lived in raucously immoral ways. Mobs roamed the streets of large cities. Violence against the weak was commonplace. After the Great Awakening and the praying and preaching of John Wesley, George Whitefield, and other godly men, God worked powerfully. Thousands of people experienced a rebirth into newness of life. The moral and spiritual culture of the country was transformed. The radical change of life in England brought purpose, value, and hope to every level of society and spared England the violent political revolution such as occurred in France.

Before the Second Great Awakening, the American frontier had become a place of godless living. Tough men who had conquered the frontier were living rough, unchurched, non-God-fearing lives. But then the spirit of God began to move in revival. A meeting was called for the Cane Ridge Meeting House in Bourbon, Kentucky. In a sparsely populated frontier, it was uncertain how many would attend. But God was already at work. To everyone's amazement, over 20,000 people showed up for the camp meeting. People gathered all over the land surrounding the small meeting house that seated only 250 people. Ministers were preaching simultaneously all over the grounds. Some people were singing, others praying, many crying out for mercy for forgiveness, while others were shouting in joy. Someone described the noise of it all as like the roar of Niagara Falls. One minister observed 500 people swept down before God under the power of conviction and then giving confession and worship to God. The frontier was radically altered. True spirituality and genuine Christianity began to describe the westward movement in our country for a while, instead of drunkenness, gambling, cursing, vice, and violence.

As sure as are God's promises and power, God can awaken the church and the world to the abundant and eternal life that he offers. God will always have the power to perform everything he has promised. In the dry wilderness of the Sinai desert, God miraculously brought water out of a rock in such abundance that it flowed like a mighty river. This river supplied enough water to quench the thirst of at least two to three million Israelites and all of their flocks. (The Bible records there were 600,000 men of fighting age not counting women and children.) Scripture says that God opened the rock, and water gushed out in the dry places like a river (Exod.17:6; Num. 20:11; Ps. 105:41). Now, that was some river! Can you imagine it? And if God can bring a river out of a rock in the wilderness enough to satisfy the thirst of several million people and their flocks, he can pour out a revival on the earth. He can release a mighty river of love into this barren world.

If we are looking for hope that God can spiritually revive his people, here's hope. If God can bring enough water from a rock to meet the needs of millions of thirsty people, this gives me hope personally. My heart is hard. But God has promised to help me and has declared that out of my *"heart will flow rivers of living water"* (John 7:38). It brings me hope for others whose hearts may seem impervious to God's call. It gives me hope for the church. I believe there is a river-releasing miracle coming in the wilderness for God's church. And I have hope for our world that can seem so closed off to God. God can flow like a mighty river through our nation and our world with his saving grace and abundant life. This river is the revival for our day that we need. We cannot be content with less than all God can do.

There is a river of life-giving water that flows from the throne of God (Rev. 22:1), through the cross of Calvary, and then through the church through the hearts of God's consecrated, revived children. This river is a surging torrent of divine love and life that is great enough to satisfy the world's thirst. Christ not only has the *power* to revive his church and awaken the world to his eternal life, but it is also his deepest *desire*. He has already proven his desire by giving his life on the cross for us. He waits to pour out his spirit in astounding abundance when we turn to him in repentance and faith.

May our heart-cry be for a mighty revival! But such a heart-cry must begin with God's revival work in each of our hearts. If we long to know God more intimately and love him more deeply, then we are longing to be revived to this fullness of his life. We also desire with God for this world to know the wonder and fulfillment of this abundant, eternal life in Christ. It does little good to look for a mighty, worldwide revival if we don't long to experience God's work in our own lives.

We can't stand back from our call to personally reach out now to bring others to the abundant life of Christ. We can't hold back from our call to Christlikeness and expect God to do all his spiritual work within us when revival comes. Our obedience now to all of God's call is a crucial key to God's future work in revival. Our negligence to hear God's call in the present will be a hindrance to the coming of the mighty revival we desire.

It is time for God to work again in a great outpouring of his spirit. Although there have been several outstanding local or regional revivals, there has been no significant, world-impacting revival in more than one hundred years. What will it take to stir us to our immense need and our answer in Christ alone? Surely our complacency in light of the urgent need is a sin before God since he has promised to respond if we seek him.

Our heart-cry for revival is nothing compared to the heart-cry of God's own heart. The cry of God's heart is for us to be revived to know him intimately and love him deeply. Oh, that we would move from indifference to a fervent desire that lives be changed, and God be glorified! Oh, that we would have a vision of what matters to God and be passionate about it! Would that we had hearts that cry out, "*Oh, that You would rend the heavens! That You would come down!*" (Isa. 64:1).

God is looking for a person or a group of people who will trust him with all their hearts, who are willing to deny themselves, take up their cross daily, follow him, and lose their lives to find them in Christ alone. God seeks those who are brokenhearted over the lost, passionately praying for heaven to open, overwhelmingly hungering for God's presence, and joyfully living for the honor of his name. When God finds such people, he will come into their lives with his presence, power, and the marvelous wonder of his working.

Will we be that person or group of people to whom God can bring such a blessing? Will we long for that which God longs? Let's hunger and thirst for it. Let's know God's heart and believe his promises. Let's pay the price of repentance, joyful obedience, and prevailing prayer. Let's take God at his Word. Let's have expectant faith. Let's not settle for less than all God has for us through his amazing grace.

How far will we let our desire to know God intimately and to love him supremely take us? Will we long for and believe for a miracle of his work? For ourselves? For those we love? For the church? For our nation and our world? Let's believe for a miracle as wondrous, and a promise as sure, as a river from a rock.

"God, revive us again. Pour water on this thirsty land. Glorify your name. May your water of life flow in the dry places like a river. May your spirit flood the nations, and your glory cover the earth."

So Longs My Soul

Chapter 22

So Longs My Soul

How can one express the inexpressible wonder of knowing God in intimate fellowship? This fellowship is our privilege and our invitation from God! Nothing else but this will satisfy the soul. Nothing else will fulfill the longing of our hearts. For this divine fellowship, God created us. To this, we are called. To this sacred relationship with God, we can choose to open our hearts.

How is this possible? How can such a wondrous thing be? This communion with God can be ours because God desires it and because Christ's work on the cross made it possible. When we separated ourselves from a holy and loving God by our sin and rebellion, removing the barrier between God and us seemed impossible. But God found a way. Christ removed the barrier by taking the judgment for our sin upon himself at Calvary. Now we can experience what God had passionately desired in his love for us all along. God knew before creation what he would do when our choices in free will would take us away from him. God planned to redeem us and win us back to himself through his sacrificial love and atoning work on the cross.

The Father, Son, and Holy Spirit have been eternally God and eternally three in one. Love has always existed as a fellowship among and between the three persons of the Trinity. This intimate, glorious dance of love and joy has eternally been the fundamental reality behind all that exists.

In his inscrutable and indescribable love, God has invited us to join the Trinity in this fellowship, this dance of everlasting life. The wonder of wonders is that God truly desires that we be a part of this intimate, consummate communion of love. There, embraced and enfolded in the perfect love of the Trinity, we experience and celebrate the eternal joy of God himself and the everlasting life he offers. How can we comprehend it? Even all of eternity will not reveal the depth of God's love for us or the marvel of his desire to share with us the interrelational life of the Godhead. What fathomless love is this?

God reached over my rebellion, atheism, and hostility to the church with his overwhelming love and drew me to himself. The revelation of God's reaching, personal love for me, and my encounter with his grace have been the greatest events in my life. Everything has changed. Everything has become new. Since God sought me out that I might find him, my deepest desire, my greatest longing, has been that I might know Christ in ever-increasing intimacy.

I know that my longing for God is just because he first longed for me and reached for me. All of our hunger, all of our seeking God, begins in his grace and his reaching for us. We love God because he first loved us. We long for him because he first longed for us in unfailing love. God seeks us to grant us forgiveness and new birth from above. Then, he calls us to an ever-increasing, intimate fellowship with himself and an ever-deeper experience of his love, his holiness, and his will. God desires that we might declare with the Apostle Paul " ... *I press on, that I may lay hold of that for which Christ Jesus has also laid hold of me*" (Phil. 3:12).

How can we describe this longing for God? Like a hunger for food when we are incredibly hungry, or a thirst for water when we are desperately thirsty, our longing for God can be urgent and gripping. This intense longing can be like a fire within us that melts our hearts and sets ablaze our fervency. Our hunger can be an aching wound in our hearts, yearning to be healed and satisfied in the Beloved's embrace, only to be smitten in that embrace all the more deeply with fervent longing. (Blessed wound!) Our thirst is for God—to know him, love him lavishly, be embraced in his ineffable, breathtaking love, and give ourselves entirely and daringly for the accomplishment of his will and the glory of his name. This longing is first for God himself—not earthly, temporal blessings, or even his spiritual gifts. We long for God and his personal, manifested presence with a pure, passionate, and unapologetic thirst.

God, who stirs us by his spirit to long for him, has promised to respond to our genuine thirst. "*For he satisfies the thirsty and fills the hungry with good things*" (Ps. 107:9 NLT). "*And Jesus said to them, 'I am the bread of life. He who comes to Me shall never hunger, and he who believes in*

Me shall never thirst'" (John 6:35). *"On the last day, that great day of the feast, Jesus stood and cried out, saying, 'If anyone thirsts, let him come to Me and drink'"* (John 7:37). *" ... I will give of the fountain of the water of life freely to him who thirsts"* (Rev. 21:6). How can we read such promises and not be stirred? How can we know that God is setting before us such an incomparable blessing and not respond with an ardent passion for experiencing all of that to which God invites us?

God responds to the cries of the spiritually hungry. God reveals himself to desperate and thirsty men and women who stand upon his promises in expectant faith. We can declare with the Psalmist, *"so pants my soul for You, O God"* (Ps. 42:1). These words of longing are not just about the writer's dependence upon God but are primarily about the overwhelming desire for God himself and the joy and pleasure of being in his presence.

But, there is even more for our hearts to take in. God's heart longs for you and me. The whole of Scripture pictures for us a God who is saying, "So longs My heart for you." We don't have to overcome God's reluctance for intimacy with us; we just need to lay hold of his highest willingness. God reaches personally and individually for each one of us. How special it is, and how blessed we are, when we receive the revelation that God seeks to reveal himself and his love to us personally!

Not long ago, I was awakened at about 4 a.m. with a deep yearning in my heart for God. My soul was overflowing with gratitude and love for Christ. My longing to embrace God with my love in prayer was overwhelming. I arose and went to my study and prayer room. My drawing to God was so great that all I could do was raise my face to heaven and sob, "Oh, God, I love you!" "I love you!" I felt a great drawing to step outside onto the deck off of my study. It was on the second story of our home and was almost like a treehouse nestled in sturdy oak trees all around. As I lifted my hands in my praise of utter abandonment to God, every tree, every star, even the breeze seemed alive with God's presence! Once again, I cried out, "Oh, God, I love you!" Just then, suddenly, a shooting star blazed across the night sky. The trees around me glowed with its light. Then, it was as if God's voice came to me through all of creation around me and, yet, personally from the heart of my God himself: "I L-o-v-e You!" The message was real and definite. God was speaking to *me*. I fell to my knees weeping, broken in my unworthiness, ecstatic in my joy, and consumed by God's love. God had awakened me in the middle of the night that we might have a holy, glorious tryst in shared love. What a wonderful God this is! This God is my God! How can one convey the wonder of God's astonishing, undeserved, fathomless, ravishing, overwhelming love?

Unworthy as we are, our hunger and thirst for God always draw him to us. God desires to be desired. The longing for God that the specially blessed saints of God possessed was what made them especially blessed. Listen to the thirst of David's heart. *"O God, You are my God; early will I seek You; my soul thirsts for You; my flesh longs for You in a dry and thirsty land where there is no water"* (Ps. 63:1). *" ... My heart and my flesh cry out for the living God"* (Ps. 84:2). *"I spread out my hands to You; my soul longs for You like a thirsty land"* (Ps. 143:6).

Our delight in God pleases him, even glorifies him. I remember holding our young son when he was only a few weeks old and talking to him as a proud father would. And then—he smiled! He smiled back at me! How delighted I was that he delighted in me! Suddenly I had a powerful, heart-melting revelation of the heart of God, of his delight in my delight in him. I realized a little of how God feels about the joy I take in him. When we supremely love God and long for fellowship with him because we delight in him, he is delighted and glorified! When we are delighted in God, that's when we most bless him, that is when we most truly glorify him.

In what will we delight? For what will we thirst? What will we love most? We are becoming what we love. Our most potent longings set the direction for our future. Our aspirations give birth to our actions. Our deepest desires determine our destiny. If we love God supremely and long to know him intimately, these are the most significant factors that will guide our choices and determine our blessings.

When we long for God, we long for what he desires. Our cherishing of God causes us to cherish what he cherishes. When we hunger for God, what matters to God matters to us. Our love for God shapes our perspective and every aspect of our Christian walk, even our faith. *" ... All that matters now is living in the faith that is activated and brought to perfection by love"* (Gal. 5:6 TPT). God desires that his children reveal him to the world. He waits for our intimate relationship with him to show his love and holiness through us to the world.

King David invites us to share his passion when he writes, *"Oh, taste and see that the Lord is good"* (Ps. 34:8). The exciting thing about this loving relationship with God is that the more we "taste" of him, the more our desire to feed upon him. This growing relationship is part of the great adventure and romance of our walk with God. There is always more to discover concerning the wonder of who he is and the fullness of his love.

We are satisfied in this life only with him, yet we are longing for more of him. We can be both satisfied and increasingly hungry at the same time. We can have overwhelming satisfaction and still have a consuming desire for more. It is a paradox, I know. We can be abundantly joyful and grateful and, yet, be desperately thirsty for more of God. We can joy in God's presence and be thankful for all he has done, and we can still be hungry for more of God's presence and his working in our lives.

God had done great things for Moses. God had heard Moses' prayer to spare the children of Israel when he had threatened to wipe them out after their rebellion. While Moses was on the mountain talking to God on their behalf, the Israelites had forsaken God. God heard Moses' prayers, and he would spare the nation, but he said that he would not go with them himself to the Promise Land. So, Moses again asked for more. He pleaded for God to go with them. Once again, God responded to the prayers of Moses. But with all of this granted by God, Moses still wasn't satisfied. Moses had the audacity to want more still. He cried out to God, *" ... Please, show me Your glory!"* (Exod. 33:18). I believe God was delighted with Moses' audacious hunger for a greater revelation of himself. God answered Moses' prayer and let him see a portion of his glory as he hid Moses in the cleft of a rock.

God is delighted in our thirst for more of him. We please him with our extravagant love and a passionate hunger for him. God knows that as we possess more of him, and he possesses more of us, we fulfill our purpose and magnify his glory.

Our spiritual thirst is crucial to our getting to an increasing fullness of our fellowship with God. How can we maintain and nurture the intensity of our spiritual desire? Even with a relationship with God being so sacred and fulfilling, we can turn away from God and become cold in our love for him. Many things vie for our hearts' devotion and can pull us away from our loving commitment to God.

However, we can choose to keep our hearts tuned to God's heart. We can nurture our longing for God until it is the greatest thing in our lives. We do this as we feed on God's Word in our regular, personal, devotional times, and as we hear it preached and exposited under the anointing. We keep our hunger for God as we pray honest, desperate, passionate, faith-filled prayers, and as we worship freely and full-heartedly alone and in oneness with other Christians. We keep our thirst for God active and acute as we obey each leading of his spirit, as we show God's love to those around us, and as we witness to others of Christ's love and saving grace.

We must guard our hunger against any un-Christlike attraction of the world and the lusts of our flesh. We must feed our souls with heavenly food, not food that only dulls our appetite for the things of God.

We can turn our hearts to God in adoring love throughout the day and tell him how we love him and how we long for him. We can be attentive to God's approach and wooing love as he calls us to worship in his presence, even in the middle of our daily activities.

Our sensitivity and response to God's approach to us are crucial to our maintaining tender and hungry hearts toward him. This openness and sensitivity to God are what has characterized all of God's consecrated servants. We want King David's longing to be our own: "*When you said, 'Seek My face,' my heart said to You, 'Your face, Lord, will I seek'*" (Ps. 27:8).

Keeping our hearts clear with God is one of the most important things we can do to maintain our growing thirst for him. In a fallen world with our fallen hearts, we can fail God in ways large and small. Because of the assurance of Christ's love, we may not feel the need to repent and stay in the clear with God. However, these disobediences can build up, blocking our vital communion with God. If we would quickly repent, we would immediately clear out the obstructions, and the rich and full fellowship with God could be restored. The Apostle John wrote explicitly to Christians, "*If we confess our sins, He is faithful and just to forgive us our sins and to cleanse us from all unrighteousness*" (1 John 1:9). If we are genuinely and overwhelmingly thirsty for God, we want nothing to ever block our sweet fellowship with him. Repentance with brokenness is a key to continual, unhindered, and growing intimacy with God. Repentance to God and hearts kept clear with others will open the door to spiritual joy in our walk with God.

We keep our passion for God ablaze as we place our hearts next to the fire of his presence. Next to his heart, the blaze of God's love ignites our hearts with holy flames of longing devotion. If we feel we have little ardent desire for God but know that we should; first, we must make sure our hearts are right with God and others by repentance. Then, we bring what desire we do have to God and ask him to multiply it. We simply ask God to stir our hearts to a passionate love for him. If we are open and sincere before God, we can pray, "Lord, give me the desire to love you passionately." If we don't have the desire to have the desire, then we can pray, "Lord, give me the desire to have the desire to love you passionately." I believe God will answer even such a prayer and meet us with this heart-changing grace.

When we seek God's face, we will discover his heart. God desires for us to seek him so that we might find him. In his lavish love for us, God bids us come and go with him on an adventure of never-ending love. God loves our devotion to him. He loves our faces and our voices. Our Beloved speaks and calls to us, "*rise up, my love, my fair one, and come away. ...let me see your face, let me hear your voice*" (Song of Sol. 2:10, 14).

God can be the single, over-riding, overwhelming obsession of our lives. Our thirst can be as the Psalmist wrote: "*As the dear pants for the water brooks, so pants my soul for You, O God. My soul thirsts for God, the living God*" (Ps. 42:1-2). Oh, to plunge into the fathomless depths of God's love! God longs for us to long for him. He calls us to thirst for him and be satisfied and then be ever thirsty for more of him and his love.

Jesus reaches in love for his church and each Christian and says, "*Behold, I stand at the door and knock. If anyone hears My voice and opens the door, I will come in to him and dine with him and he with Me*"

(Rev. 3:20). Jesus, himself, stands at the door of our hearts and asks to enter for intimate communion. The offer is God's. The choice is ours.

God's love is an unfailing love that will not let us go as we drink fully from the waters of his life. The spirit of God still calls us to the fountain of living water: " ...*'Come!' And let him who thirsts come. Whoever desires, let him take the water of life freely"* (Rev. 22:17). The promise of God still is ours to claim: *"For I will pour water on him who is thirsty, and floods on the dry ground"* (Isa. 44:3).

Jesus told the woman at the well in Samaria, *"whoever drinks of the water that I shall give him will never thirst. But the water that I shall give him will become in him a fountain of water springing up into everlasting life"* (John 4:14). I would reply as did that God-sought woman 2,000 years ago. "Sir, give me this water." So pants my longing soul for God.

Rod Taylor is available for book interviews and personal appearances. For more information contact:

Rod Taylor
C/O Advantage Books
P.O. Box 160847
Altamonte Springs, FL 32716
info@advbooks.com

To purchase additional copies of these books, visit our bookstore at:
www.advbookstore.com

Longwood, Florida, USA
"we bring dreams to life"™
www.advbookstore.com